Enjoy
Exploring!

Linda
Taylor

Great Women Exploring Nature
How Wild Florida Influenced Their Lives

Linda Taylor

authorHOUSE®

AuthorHouse™
1663 Liberty Drive, Suite 200
Bloomington, IN 47403
www.authorhouse.com
Phone: 1-800-839-8640

First published by AuthorHouse 4/1/2008

ISBN: 978-1-4343-4308-6 (sc)

Library of Congress Control Number: 2008902936

Printed in the United States of America
Bloomington, Indiana

This book is printed on acid-free paper.

Cover: "21 Palms" oil painting by Bill Renc, Copyright © 2008 by Bill Renc.

Dedication

To my mother, Mona Taylor, who preordered the first copy of GWEN ten years ago continuing to encourage me through her words, actions, and love.

To my father, John Taylor, who inspires me every day with his love, acceptance, kindness and generosity.

Introduction

Who Is GWEN? She may be in you.

GWEN—Great Women Exploring Nature

As you meet the women of GWEN, you will learn that nature encourages us to rise beyond self. The ecology of the natural world inspires us to explore the ecology of our soul. Throughout history women have felt the cycles of nature parallel their own. Many cultures honored the intuitive wisdom that women cultivated from their understanding of Mother Earth. This connection faded as society drifted from the lessons of nature into the industrial and then the technical age. At different points in history, the women of GWEN sought to reconnect to this powerful teacher in their own way.

The common landscape of GWEN is the natural world of Florida. I was drawn to this theme as I became aware of how my own relocation to this dense tropical state had affected my state of mind. Many of these women will be familiar. Perhaps their personalities and yearnings parallel your own. You may be surprised to learn about their connection to the sandy shores and wild land of the Sunshine State. As you become familiar with their place in history, you will also see intriguing connections of one to another.

This book evolved from a tiny slip of paper I called a GWEN fact. Guiding women on nature awareness walks, I would slip these tidbits of knowledge into lunch bags. As we sat on the beach or in the woods eating our snack, each woman would share the GWEN fact she found in her brown bag. Faces glowed as they read out loud about a woman of history with feelings similar to their own. The magic of such moments inspired me to expand GWEN's information. But to my surprise, I discovered a personal conflict as I dived into the research to expose more of each woman's life. I felt intrusive. It was similar to how I guided our excursions into the wild.

I did not want us to get too close. I encouraged us to blend and just use our senses to feel. I provided enough information to add to the encounter, but left the mystery of the plant, rock, or animal to the moment. I know from my own experience the intimacy one can feel toward the shorebirds, a dolphin, or the wind in a pine is not for interpretation by another. How it inspires me changes with each circumstance.

My hope is that GWEN will shine on your own path. This book will guide you to the places that spoke to these women. Give yourself an experience beyond the words, and walk the earth they walked. Clear your mind in the outdoor world to feel the messages that spoke to their soul. Smell the forests and salty air that quieted their thoughts. See the landscapes that guided their lives. When you allow your body to move gently in the rhythm of nature, a new world may appear before your eyes.

You may just discover your own Cross Creek as Marjorie Kinnan Rawlings did at a crossroad in her life. Something inspired Rachel Carson to find the courage to describe to the world how close we were to a Silent Spring. Anne Morrow Lindbergh was guided to find the perfect experience on which to reflect before writing a book of inspiration that has touched generations. Mina Miller Edison and Marjorie Harris Carr vigorously supported activism for wildlife and the land and gained power through the support of their husbands and families. You can inspire generations in a local area, such as Myrtle Scharrer Betz did when, at the age of eighty-seven, she wrote down her memories of living on Caladesi Island. You can demand that the world pay attention to the Everglades as Marjory Stoneman Douglas did into her 100s. If you look beyond your ego, the horizon gets bigger. As you use your senses to really feel the experience of walking on the beach or sitting in the woods, you will feel the wonder of nature. Learn from her wisdom.

The women of GWEN are as different as us all. Some were from privilege, others from extreme poverty. Historians still probe the mystery that surrounds aspects of their lives. Supportive partners ranged from husbands to mothers to friends. Most had complicated lives filled with both happiness and despair.

I have added environmental and historical tidbits to fill in the richness of the moment. History helps us understand what is happening in our own lives as it relates to circumstances in our environment.

I am grateful for the talent and wisdom of Linda Renc, an artistic woman who has shared many nature adventures with me. A renowned calligrapher, Linda took her talent to another level as she sketched natural elements into the GWEN quotes that related to each woman's connection to her place. Her insightful map of Florida pulls together the connections to the land. Linda guided me to her husband Bill Renc's work. "21 Palms" perfectly captures the soulful song of a wild Florida that spoke to the GWEN women ...... but that is disappearing fast.

I am also inspired by the remarkable spirit of Terry Fortner, the granddaughter of Myrtle Scharrer Betz. Terry has dedicated much of her life to documenting the history of her family, evidence of how honoring our own plot of land can make such a difference.

On another note, I was challenged with the task of making this book as sustainable as possible. Publishing in controlled quantities through AuthorHouse who uses a very green-focused printer, Lightning Source, gave me that opportunity.

If we find our own rhythm, a movement that is reflected in the natural world around us, we can redefine our self and purpose. Nature helps us discover the brightness of our spirit and shines it on our lives, our relationships, and our deeds.

Thank you for taking the time to meet the women of GWEN. You just may get to know yourself a little better.

Table of Contents

Great Women Exploring Nature

Harriet Beecher Stowe

Mina Miller Edison

Marjory Stoneman Douglas

Zora Neale Hurston

Myrtle Scharrer Betz

Marjorie Kinnan Rawlings

Anne Morrow Lindbergh

Jackie Cochran

Rachel Carson

Marjorie Harris Carr

Harriet Beecher Stowe

June 14, 1811 (Litchfield, Connecticut)–July 1, 1896 (Hartford, Connecticut)

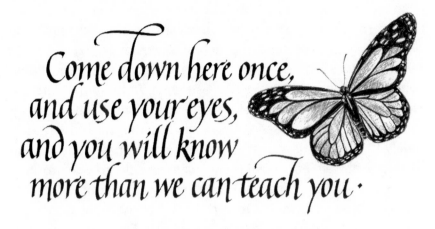

Come down here once, and use your eyes, and you will know more than we can teach you.

Harriet Beecher Stowe

Harriet Beecher Stowe shaped her place in history when she courageously expanded a short story about the death of an old slave into a novel that captivated both sides of the Atlantic Ocean. *Uncle Tom's Cabin*, also known as *Life Among the Lowly*, written in 1852 by Harriet Beecher Stowe, is considered one of the most influential books of modern history. Later in her life, Harriet became Florida's first travel writer, exposing the people of the North to the wild nature of her winter home. "Oranges from Harriet Beecher Stowe, Mandarin, Florida" stamped on crates shipped north beckoned the adventurous.

On June 14, 1811, in the town of Litchfield, Connecticut, Reverend Lyman Beecher and Roxana Foote Beecher announced the birth of their seventh child. Neither of these passionate Federalists could have imagined that this tiny girl would one day preach a sermon that would reach the entire country and beyond. Harriet's parents instilled both the love of education and the courage to fight for one's conviction in all twelve of their children.

Harriet's character was molded by a strong connection to the natural world around her. The rare beauty of the hills, woods, and streams of Litchfield, Connecticut, cultivated her lifelong love of nature. Of this impression she says, "My earliest recollections of Litchfield are those of its beautiful scenery, which impressed and formed my mind long before I had words to give names to my emotions, or could analyze my mental processes."

Harriet was first a student and then a teacher at an educational institution founded by her sister Catherine. At the time, Hartford Female Seminary was one of only a handful of schools that took the education of girls seriously. In 1832, Harriet moved with her family to Cincinnati, where her father became president of Lane Theological Seminary. Cincinnati was considered the frontier, but also a hotbed of the abolitionist movement. Four years later, Harriet married Calvin Stowe, a professor at the seminary. Six of their seven children were born while living in Cincinnati, a city just across the river from Kentucky, a slave state. Harriet first became aware of the horrors of slavery after discovering that their servant, Zillah, was actually a runaway slave. Harriet learned intimately from Zillah of the unspeakable horrors endured by the enslaved African people. Harriet's husband drove Zillah to the next station on the Underground Railroad. Observations, such as a young woman running across the ice on the river with her baby clutched to her chest, moved Harriet to the scenes she developed in *Uncle Tom's Cabin*.

Harriet's writing spanned fifty-one years and produced thirty volumes of novels, stories, sketches, and poems. She was fortunate to have the support of her husband, Calvin. This kind of encouragement was unusual at a time when women were not expected to have a career outside the home. In a letter Calvin wrote her in 1840, he said, "my dear, you must be a literary woman. It is so written in the book of fate. ... Make all your calculations accordingly."

In 1850, Harriet's husband joined the faculty of his alma mater, Bowdoin College in Brunswick, Maine. The Stowe family moved to Maine, where Harriet began her work on a serial story in an abolitionist newspaper, the *National Era*. The story was inspired by her distress over the Fugitive Slave Act of 1850, which made it a crime for citizens of free states to give aid to runaway enslaved people. Harriet's sister-in-law wrote her, saying, "Harriet, if I could use a pen as you can, I would write something that would make this whole nation feel what an accursed thing slavery is." After reading this aloud to her children, Harriet dramatically crumpled the paper in her hand and said, "I will write something if I live." While at church, she is said to have had a vision of "Uncle Tom's death" and was reportedly moved to tears. She immediately went home and started to pen the words that were destined to change the world.

Her powerful writing about the life of southern slaves caused a tremendous stir among the magazine's readers. Harriet instinctively addressed *Uncle Tom's Cabin* to the people of the South and honestly thought it a hand held out for peace. Her writing humanized slavery by telling the story of individuals and families. Harriet portrayed the physical, sexual, and emotional abuse endured by enslaved people. When she created the character of Eliza Harris, the slave mother, she drew from her own experiences. Her son, Samuel Charles, "Charley," died of cholera when he was still an infant. Harriet could identify deeply with the feelings surrounding the loss of a child as she wrote about a mother losing her child in a slavery sales transaction. She did believe if the South could see slavery in its stark reality, it would voluntarily free its slaves.

A young Boston publisher, John Jewett, made overtures for the publication in book form long before it was finished as a serial. The announcement of the publication occurred on March 20, 1852. Jewett expressed fear that Harriet was making the story too long for one volume. He reminded her that the subject was unpopular, and that one short volume might possibly sell, but two volumes could prove fatal to the success of the book. Harriet replied that she did not make the story, the story made itself, and that she could not stop till it was done.

Jewett offered her either 10 percent on all sales or half the profit with half the risk in case the venture proved unprofitable. Harriet and her husband turned to a business adviser, Phillip Greeley, then a member of Congress. Without reading the story, he strongly advised them to accept the 10 percent on all sales and to take no risk. He reasoned that the subject was very unpopular, and a book written by a woman could not be expected to have a very large sale success. Also, there had never been a major American novel with an African American hero. Professor Stowe placed the first copy of the first edition into Phillip's hands at the railroad station just as his train was to depart. Phillip began reading *Uncle Tom's Cabin* and discovered that he could not put down the book or stop tears in his eyes. On arriving at his destination, he went to his room and stayed up all night to finish reading the story that would affect the world in this same way.

Harriet had hoped "it would make enough so I may have a silk dress." Three thousand copies of *Uncle Tom's Cabin* sold the day of publication; 10,000 were sold in a few days and 20,000 in three weeks. Within a year, more than 300,000 copies were sold. Eight power presses running night and day barely kept up with the demand. It was a best seller in the United States, Europe, and Asia, and by 1854 was translated into sixty languages. Harriet became America's first female novelist and toured Europe in 1853. The indignation, pity, and distress that had long weighed on her soul seemed to pass from her to her readers.

Another major theme of *Uncle Tom's Cabin* is the moral power of women. Through characters like Eliza, who escapes from slavery to save her young son and eventually reunites her entire family, or Little Eva, who is seen as the "ideal Christian," Harriet shows her belief that women are capable of saving those around them from even the worst injustices. While later critics have noted that her female characters are often domestic clichés instead of realistic women, Harriet's writing affirms the importance of women's influence and helped pave the way for the women's rights movement in the following decades.

Until the actual publication in June of 1852, *Uncle Tom's Cabin* had been a controversial series, circulating as freely in the South as in the North. Harriet delved deeply into the national issue of slavery, exposing both the view from the agricultural South and the industrialized North. Her book was not just a novel, but also a powerful movement cracking the foundations of the republic. The South banned *Uncle Tom's Cabin* and arrested anyone in

possession of it. Harriet wrote that suddenly both sides perceived how powerfully it affected every mind it touched and both sides saw the truth. The breaking point of this tension occurred in South

Carolina on April 12, 1861, when the Confederate States of America attacked the 1st U.S. Artillery at Fort Sumter in the Charleston harbor. Her impact is often emphasized in the commonly quoted statement attributed to Abraham Lincoln when he met Harriet Beecher Stowe, "So you're the little woman that started this great war!"

In 1865, the Confederacy collapsed after Lee surrendered to Grant; four million slaves were freed. In the fall of the next year, Calvin and Harriet heard remarkable accounts from two Connecticut farmers regarding the merits of working the land in Florida. The Stowe's son, Frederick, had returned from the war with an extremely painful wound received during the Battle of Gettysburg. He could not resume his medical studies, as the pain drove him to the verge of insanity. Fred also suffered from alcoholism. Harriet held a very unusual and modern view of alcoholism as an illness rather than a moral failure, which was the common belief of that time. Harriet and Calvin decided that a healthful outdoor life, combined with the responsibility of making a success of an old cotton plantation, might help Fred. Although it was a purchase they could not afford, their business decisions were always guided by what good would be achieved more than the possibility of commercial success. This philosophy brought them financial burdens throughout their lives; despite the extraordinary popularity of Harriet's books, her earnings were not great, and her generosity exceeded her business savvy.

Frederick began writing to his mother from Laurel Grove, located on the west side of St. Johns River, near the town of Orange Park and not far from Jacksonville. He captured her deep adoration of nature in his description of the exquisite flowers, birds, and brilliant sunshine. For writing, Harriet wanted warm weather and soon she traveled south. Here she found a paradise at her door: cutover pinewoods known as the scrub and the St. Johns, with its unique inland sea running through it. White sand covered the floor of the woods. Enormous live oaks, half hidden in gray Spanish moss, lined the banks of the big river. Across from Orange Park was the town of Mandarin. Rowing with her son across the river to get their mail, Harriet discovered a village largely settled by people from England, under what were and still are perhaps the largest live oak trees in America, trees with overhead spreads of 135 feet and trunks 7 feet in diameter. Harriet saw a place for sale, which captivated her. It was a small cottage under one of the largest oaks looking down the broadest and straightest corridor of the St. Johns. In the rear clearing was a "great wild park" of oaks and an orange grove loading the air with the perfume of the fruit blossoms. Harriet had not dreamed of such beauty. In 1867 she purchased thirty acres on a bluff overlooking the St. Johns River for her winter residence. She called this slice of paradise "calm isle of Patmos."

A love affair between the land and this enterprising woman glowed in her letters. She wrote of the five large date palms, fragrant orange grove, and magnificent olive tree. But what drew her into her soulful essays was the incredible wildness of this land.

Harriet was working on another of her great novels, *Oldtown Folks*. To the disapproval of her publisher, she traveled to Mandarin and remained silent in her writing for three months. Unknown to many, she had found Laurel Grove Plantation demoralized and Fred wretched in his addiction. Harriet had put $10,000 into the investment, and it had yet to market its first bale of cotton. After trying to manage and reorganize the plantation herself, she soon took Fred north and returned to finishing *Oldtown Folks*. Fred left for California and was never heard from again. Harriet found a responsible partner in her cousin to help her manage her Mandarin orange grove. Soon this fruit farm flourished with orange crates labeled "Oranges from Harriet Beecher Stowe, Mandarin, Florida" heading for northern markets.

In 1870, Harriet returned to Mandarin and continued to enlarge her cottage to accommodate her entire family. In the winter of 1872, she offered a series of essays to the *Christian Union* under the title of *Palmetto Leaves*. Vividly describing the land and people in her sketches, Harriet had created what is considered the first promotional travel writing for Florida. Besides giving an intimate glimpse of her own life in Mandarin, Harriet painted a picture of Florida as a tropical paradise, which remained a Northern impression until railroads and the automobile opened up the state as a winter playground. The *Palmetto Leaves* sketches were published as a book in 1873. Harriet wrote that 14,000 Northern tourists had visited Florida that year, many of them no doubt drawn southward by her writing. She welcomed tourists debarking from the steamers and charged each seventy-five cents to meet her and admire her surroundings. She told readers that Florida was like a piece of embroidery with two sides to it, "one side all rag-tag and threads without order or position; the other showing flowers and brilliant colors." The topics in *Palmetto Leaves* included adventures in the woods with flowers, trees, and birds; her observations of former slaves finding their way in freedom; projected enterprises in farms and dairies; and her deep affection for the St. Johns River. Throughout the pieces, whatever the topic, her readers felt the refreshing awareness of this Connecticut Yankee in a land she marveled. In her piece titled "Our Florida Plantation," she writes, "It was a hazy, dreamy, sultry February day, such as comes down from the skies of Florida in the opening of spring. A faint scent of orange blossoms was in the air, though as yet there seemed to be only white buds on the trees. The deciduous forest along the banks of the broad St. Johns was just showing that misty dimness which announces the opening of young buds. The river lay calm as a mirror, streaked here and there with broad bands of intense blue which melted into purplish mist in the distance."

Harriet's work also captured the culture of the people who were populating this southern frontier and her involvement in advocating for their rights. In Mandarin, she established schools for the children of former slaves. She also fostered the development of an ecumenical church. In 1870, she started an integrated school in Mandarin for children and adults. This was an early step toward providing equal education in the area and predated the national movement toward integration by more than a half century.

Harriet Beecher Stowe's long and productive life ended at the age of eighty-five on July 1, 1896, at her home in Connecticut. She blended her love of the human essence and the natural world into a legacy that helped shape the world we know today. She will always remain in history as one of our greatest heroes.

Thank you Harriet Beecher Stowe for your ability to write about the human condition and the natural world with such detail and insight, causing readers to stop, take notice, and act.

Did you know?

Federalist—Someone loyal to the Union Army during the U.S. Civil War.

Underground Railroad—A network of secret routes and safe houses that African slaves used to escape to free states or as far north as Canada, with the aid of abolitionists (those who sought to put an end to slavery).

Scrub—An endangered Florida ecosystem found on coastal and inland sand ridges and is characterized by a plant community dominated by shrubs, dwarf oaks, and sandpines.

Live Oak—The name live oak comes from the fact that evergreen oaks are still green and alive in winter, when other oaks are dormant, leafless, and dead-looking. The live oak grows forty to eighty feet tall with crown spreading to one hundred feet wide. Live oak was widely used in early American shipbuilding.

Spanish Moss—Spanish moss is not biologically related to moss. Instead, it is a flowering plant in the bromeliads family that grows hanging from tree branches in full sun or partial shade. It ranges from the southeastern United States to South America, growing wherever the climate is warm enough and there is relatively high average humidity. Propagation primarily occurs when fragments blow on the wind and stick to tree limbs, or are carried by birds as nesting material. Spanish moss is an epiphyte, not a parasite.

Patmos—A small Greek island in the Aegean Sea. Patmos is most notable for its mention in the Christian scriptural Book of Revelation.

Explore the Land that Influenced Harriet Beecher Stowe

St. Johns River

The St. Johns River is the longest river in Florida, stretching 310 miles from Indian River County to the Atlantic Ocean in Duval County. It flows generally north and is designated as one of the American Heritage Rivers. Many parks exist along this magical river.

Web Site: www.sjr.state.fl.us

References and Recommended Readings

Web Site: www.harrietbeecherstowecenter.org

The May Flower, 1843, by Harriet Beecher Stowe.

Uncle Tom's Cabin, 1852, by Harriet Beecher Stowe.

A Key to Uncle Tom's Cabin, 1853, by Harriet Beecher Stowe.

Dred: A Tale of the Great Dismal Swamp, 1856, by Harriet Beecher Stowe.

The Minister's Wooing, 1859, by Harriet Beecher Stowe.

The Pearl of Orr's Island, 1862, by Harriet Beecher Stowe.

Oldtown Folks, 1869 by Harriet Beecher Stowe.

Palmetto Leaves, 1873, by Harriet Beecher Stowe.

Harriet Beecher Stowe: The Story of Her Life, 1889, Charles Stowe (her son).

Crusader in Crinoline: The Life of Harriet Beecher Stowe, 1941, by Forrest Wilson.

Harriet Beecher Stowe, 1989, by John Adams.

The Limits of Sisterhood: The Beecher Sisters on Women's Rights and Women's Sphere, 1988, by Jeanne Boydston, Mary Kelley, Anne Margolis.

The Oxford Harriet Beecher Stowe Reader, 1999, by Joan D. Hedrick.

Mina Miller Edison

July 6, 1865 (Akron, Ohio)–August 24, 1947 (New York, New York)

There is nothing that is more life giving than a tree.

Mina Miller Edison

Mina Edison loved gardens, trees, and birds. She possessed a unique insight: understanding the connection between gardens, family, and community. Mina and Thomas Edison, along with their son Theodore, were pioneers of environmental protection in Florida. They fought the shameful slaughter of egrets and parakeets for the millinery trade. Mina Edison proved to be an influential voice in the development of gardens and the preservation of trees throughout southwest Florida.

In 1885, Thomas Edison chose Fort Myers, a settlement in the outback of Florida, as his winter home.. Edison, then thirty-eight, discovered this wilderness town while traveling with Ezra Gilliland, a friend from Thomas's early days as a telegrapher. Searching for the perfect material to make a uniform carbon filament for his incandescent lamp, Thomas explored the Caloosahatchee River. Intrigued by the bamboo growing tall, he followed it up the river and found Fort Myers. This sleepy town was difficult to reach and certainly not on the sandy shores of the railroad-accessible east coast. Thomas's first wife, Mary Stillwell, had died in the summer of the previous year, leaving him with the care of their three children. Looking for a retreat to rest from the demands of his life and business in New Jersey, this remote area of Florida felt appealing. Both Thomas and Ezra fell in love with the quiet little village and together purchased land far from the busy center of town, a mile and one-half down a cattle trail. They planned to build their homes along the river and include a laboratory so that Thomas Edison could have "working" vacations.

In the same year Ezra introduced Thomas to the wilds of Fort Myers, he also introduced him to Mina Miller at a dinner party. Thomas first saw the twenty-year-old dark-haired woman when she accompanied her father, Lewis, at an agricultural exposition. Although Edison's young daughter Dot kept steering her father toward blond women who looked more like her late mother Mary, Thomas was deeply touched each time he had the pleasure of Mina's company.

Edison's love for his new jungle paradise softened his grief, allowing a great love to develop for Mina. After formally asking for her hand in marriage, they wed on February 14, 1886, and that night boarded a train to their Florida honeymoon. Mina shared Thomas's attention to not only his work but the evolution of their Florida winter home. She soon became involved in the design and implementation of an earthly paradise in the land of flowers. The Edisons decided to call their winter home Seminole Lodge after the only American Indians never conquered by the government. They wanted to show honor and sympathy to the few remaining Indians who had been driven to the remote swamps of the Everglades.

Mina's interest in nature developed when, as a young girl, she spent summers at Chautauqua Lake in southwestern New York State. Mina and her ten siblings were raised in society and affluence. The Chautauqua Assembly set a standard for education in America in an era when school was not mandatory. This Methodist training center, cofounded by Mina's father, not only gave instruction in religious and cultural matters but also offered nature walks and a very active Bird and Tree Club.

Due to a falling out with Ezra Gilliland, Thomas and Mina did not visit their Fort Myers retreat for fourteen years. By 1906, the Edisons had purchased the Gilliland home and made renovations to both sites; they again began spending winters at Seminole Lodge. Mina and Thomas had three children, Madeleine, Charles, and Theodore, in addition to the three children Thomas had by his first wife, Marion, Thomas, and William. The family loved boat trips. They traveled up the winding Caloosahatchee River to the mysterious waters of Lake Okeechobee by way of the Everglades. Mina had a keen interest in the flocks of birds that seemed to float in the air and disappear as they landed in the tall sawgrass. The family often ventured seaward to San Carlos Bay and the barrier islands of Sanibel and Captiva to participate in one of Thomas's favorite pastimes—fishing. Mina observed the changes occurring as people began to claim the wild land. She commented early on how fishing may have been spoiled for all time by dredging "improvements". Thomas was also vocal regarding the decline of tarpon caused by the net fishermen depriving the mullet and other small fish of their natural feeding grounds.

Seminole Lodge was where friends who shared their love of wildlife joined Mina and Thomas. This included naturalist John Burroughs and Henry Ford, the automobile industrialist. Henry Ford was not only the embodiment of industrial mass production but also an avid bird and nature lover. John Burroughs, author, poet, and apostle of Emerson and Thoreau, was enthralled with the birdlife of the Edison's paradise in Fort Myers. This love of birds and nature bound the friendship of the Edisons and Fords with John Burroughs. A greatly anticipated camping trip into the Everglades included Mina and the children. The camping party employed local guides to take them through the sand pines into the palmettos to set up camp by a lake sixty miles into the Everglades. The experience proved so profound that two of the Edison children wrote eloquently of this camping expedition years later. The Fords, so captivated by the beauty of Edison's jungle, soon purchased the property adjacent to theirs.

It was Henry Ford who wrote to Mina about the pending bill in Congress to protect the birds from the millinery trade slaughter. He urged Mina to encourage her famous husband to give interviews to newspapers endorsing the immediate passage of this greatly needed measure. Gathering and selling wild-bird plumes in Florida had become a very lucrative business. Hunters killed the birds during breeding season when the feathers were most beautiful; the destruction was multiplied by leaving baby birds exposed in their nests. In 1887, nearly 40 percent of all products exported from Fort Myers were bird plumes, alligator, panther, and bearskins. President Theodore Roosevelt attempted to protect the birds by assigning wardens to the rookeries. Two wardens in Florida were murdered at the hands of relentless hunters. Seeing this trade firsthand touched the hearts of the Edison family.

Both Thomas and Mina were extremely concerned about the environment around them. They realized that their refuge in southern Florida was threatened by exploitation. Mina Edison was a fervent member of the national Audubon Society, which was instrumental in protecting endangered birds. She fought tirelessly to stop the possible disappearance of the white egret, herons, and roseate spoonbills, but it was too late to stop the extinction of the Carolina parakeet. Mina also supported the Florida Federation of Women's Clubs. Both of these organizations promoted the establishment of the Royal Palm State Park, forty-five miles southwest of Miami, in the middle of the Everglades. The area is still the home to 140 different species of birds, rare butterflies, tropical snails, and 260 varieties of plants. Mina and her friends wanted the plants and animals in this area to be saved. They asked the state to set aside land as a state park. In 1916, Henry Flagler's third wife, Mary Lily Kenan gave Mina's organization 960 acres and the state of Florida matched the gift with another 960. In 1921, the state of Florida gave another 2,080 acres. Royal Palm State Park became the forerunner for the Everglades National Park.

In Mina's early years in Fort Myers, she avoided most society and civic activities in an effort to recharge from her demanding role in New Jersey. This changed around 1920, when she not only became involved but developed into an activist. Unleashing a tremendous amount of energy, one of her first crusades involved a concrete bridge slated to span her beloved Caloosahatchee. She expressed that it would demise the aesthetics of the town center. In 1928, she founded the Round Table, comprised of members of combined civic associations urging a unified effort from Rotary, Chamber of Commerce, and women's clubs toward beautification and preservation of their area. She embraced the cooperation of the black community to beautify school grounds and neighborhoods, a social landmark for that time in history. Marjorie Stoneman Douglas wrote in *McCall's* magazine that Mina Edison's founding and nurturing of the Round Table ought to be recognized as an outstanding civic achievements, "since it is an achievement, not just in the material improvements of the city but in the building up of a most amazing and creative community spirit." Her Round Table tackled the subject of restricting the cutting of trees within the town as it developed. She dedicated her energy to educating the public on forest conservation and how the beauty of Fort Myers depended on its foliage.

She shared her passion for birds by taking Girl Scouts on an all-day trip to the pelican rookery and spoke at many functions on the importance of birds. Mina was in great demand to speak, even by the Business and Professional Women's Clubs, a surprise considering Mina had expressed publicly that she deplored wives and mothers in the business field. She also brought well-known naturalists to the area to speak at various events including Dr. John K. Small, curator of the Bronx Botanical Gardens, botanist and accomplished plant explorer. In 1928, Mina stepped in to read a paper by Dr. Small who had to leave prior to the February 29 meeting of the Fort Myers Woman's Club. The presentation was titled "Trees of Florida" and focused on the astonishing fact that a large and varied tree population existed naturally in Florida, which has such a comparatively minimal diversity of surface, altitude, and climate. At the conclusion of Dr. Small's information, Mina said, "After hearing this paper does it not strike an urgent call in every heart to make a decided and rapid move to preserve our State trees? Please make this one of your greatest aims and get everyone in authority to help you before it is too late for there is nothing that is more life giving than a tree." With that she read Joyce Kilmer's poem "Trees," written in 1913.

Mina was a gardening enthusiast. Her favorite community involvement was the garden clubs. The Plant Guild, which met at Seminole Lodge, was responsible for cleanup and beautification of assigned areas. Her vision was that "the city would be fragrant with flowers from every home ... and adequate care for birds so that they too would be loath to leave." She had a deep belief that beauty was manifest in nature itself.

Mina advocated that gardens blend community work with home life, which every school, church, and home should cultivate. She was passionate that, when all members of a family become interested in the garden, a home is stabilized, making it more than just a place to sleep and eat. She felt that gardens "cover so much of nature's work which is so needed in all our lives, to soften the commercial spirit of the day. It includes air, grass, trees, shrubs, flowers, birds, in fact everything in nature—each one a study and a joy in itself."

Mina encouraged the growing of vegetables and fruits to be preserved and used throughout the year. "After the labor one can sit in the midst of all this beauty and commune with oneself while the bird adds to the charm of it all with its song, sprightliness and color." Mina believed that curiosity of our natural world starts with simple observations in a garden. "It is like finding a new world to one who learns to love the bird." She encouraged the sharing of this awareness and connection with a companion who may not have noticed the song of a bird or the flowers along the road. "There is a pride and a joy in being able to give a friend a flower out of ones own garden, to give the name of it and how to cultivate it." Mina Edison believed and lived her passion for gardens, advocating that working outdoors in a garden, using one's hands and breathing fresh air, causes one to forget their cares, unites family, and builds community "creating charm, happiness and love." During the span of more than fifty years, the Edisons created one of the most magnificent tropical gardens in the United States.

Inspired by Harvey Firestone and perhaps by Mina's passion for plant life, at the age of seventy-six, Thomas Edison devoted his remaining years to finding a domestic source of rubber. The world's premier inventor turned his mind toward botany as he experimented with the goldenrod plant at Seminole Lodge.

Sixteen years after Thomas's death in 1931, Mina decided on a priceless gift. She donated Seminole Lodge, the grounds, and the laboratory to the city of Fort Myers to be operated as a memorial to Thomas A. Edison. Mina Miller Edison died later that year, on August 24, 1947. Before her death, she described herself as the daughter, wife, and mother of inventors.

Thank you Mina, for your vision to know that our planet can be saved one garden at a time.

Did you know?

Sawgrass—A large sedge with a worldwide distribution in tropical and temperate regions. These are plants characterized by long, narrow (grass-like) leaves with sharp, often serrated (sawtooth-like) margins, and flowering stems, one to three feet tall, and bearing a much-branched inflorescence. A well-known area of extensive sawgrass growth is the Florida Everglades; sawgrass is the plant referred to by the descriptor, "River of Grass." Across the Everglades, sawgrass occurs in patches of dense growth surrounded by areas of very sparse growth. Consequently, the dense sawgrass beds harbor little animal life, but in the Everglades are the habitat used by alligators to build nests.

Tarpon—A large coastal fish. They grow up to eight feet in length and sometimes weigh 200 pounds. When swimming in oxygen-poor water, tarpons can breathe air from the surface.

John Burroughs—An American naturalist and writer important in the evolution of the U.S. conservation movement.

Millinery Trade—The profession of designing, making, trimming, and selling women's hats.

Explore the Land that Influenced Mina Edison

Edison and Ford Winter Estates, Fort Myers—Southwestern Florida

Web Site: www.efwefla.org/home.asp

References and Recommended Readings

Uncommon Friends: Life of Thomas Edison, Henry Ford, Harvey Firestone, Alexis Carrel and Charles Lindbergh, 1989, by James D. Newton.

Edison in Florida ... The Green Laboratory, 1997, by Olav Thulesius.

The Edisons of Fort Myers, 2004, by Tom Smoot.

Marjory Stoneman Douglas

April 7, 1890 (Minneapolis, Minnesota)–May 14, 1998 (Coconut Grove, Florida)

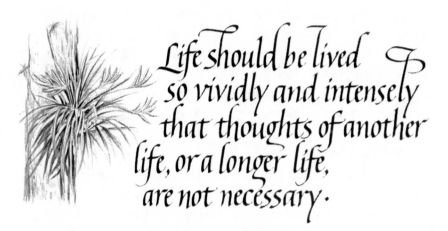

Life should be lived so vividly and intensely that thoughts of another life, or a longer life, are not necessary.

Marjory Stoneman Douglas

Marjory Stoneman Douglas's passionate relationship with the Florida Everglades developed through her research for a book she was commissioned to write. Her masterpiece, *The Everglades: River of Grass*, captured the attention of the world. Marjory's ability to explain the ecological importance of what many considered a worthless swamp was unparalleled. President Harry Truman declared the Everglades a national park soon after her book was published in 1947. Marjory Stoneman Douglas was a feminist, civil rights activist, and environmentalist long before these causes were popular. Each passion fueled the next until at the age of seventy-nine, she began her greatest and best- known career as "Defender of the Everglades."

Marjory Stoneman was born on April 7, 1890, in Minneapolis, Minnesota. At the age of four, her parents, Frank and Lillian Stoneman, took her by train to New Orleans and on to Tampa by steamer before traveling to Havana. Sights, smells, and sounds

23

imprinted a tropical wonderland on Marjory's young spirit. She recalls being held up to pick an orange from a tree in the garden of the Tampa Bay Hotel built by Henry Plant. For Marjory, the tropic light that contrasted so vividly to the dark gray Northern sky would welcome her back when she eventually returned.

Not long after that memorable trip to paradise, Marjory's mother, suffering from mental illness, took her young daughter and left her husband. Lillian and little Marjory traveled to live with her grandparents and extended family in Taunton, Massachusetts. Young Marjory experienced the confusion of observing her mother's nervous breakdown as well as the bewilderment of losing her father.

Marjory and Lillian grew close. Marjory took on the role of caring for her mother. Despite the financial difficulties with her grandfather's brass foundry, Marjory's grandmother and her aunt Fanny saw to it that Marjory have the opportunity to go to college. Through her aunt's secret savings account and her grandmother's contribution from her household fund, Marjory was sent to Wellesley College. She blossomed at the all-women's school run by accomplished women academics. With so many men killed in the Civil War and many moving West, her life had been very female focused. She experienced economics, philosophy, mathematics, and the importance of articulation. With ancestors who were leaders in the Underground Railroad, this young woman felt at home in a progressive environment. Here Marjory experienced what would form her activist passions from the suffrage movement to the excitement of observing the migration of the myrtle warblers.

Even with such a world of enlightenment surrounding her, it was hard to escape the pain of her beloved but troubled mother. Lillian had developed breast cancer, which had metastasized to her spine. Marjory's mother died soon after her graduation from Wellesley. Searching for a way to run from the pain, she followed a classmate to St. Louis, shared an apartment, and found work in a department store. When her friend returned home, Marjory found another job at Bamberger's in Newark, New Jersey. It was here she met Kenneth Douglas, a man thirty years her senior, who gave her the first attention she had ever received from a man. Three months after meeting him in 1914, they married.

Marjory's husband was a reporter who focused on uncovering vice in Newark. He apparently exposed more corruption than officials wanted and was arrested. When Kenneth was sentenced to prison, Marjory's friends and family begged her to leave this shame of a man. Marjory insisted she would stand by him. Soon after his release in 1915, she joined him in New York City and found herself dominated by Kenneth's misguided search for a livelihood.

Marjory had been left at the home of a retired minister, while Kenneth disappeared in search of work. One day her father's brother, Edward, whom she had never met, surprised her with a visit, stating that he wanted to get to know her. Unknowingly Marjory had signed bank drafts with her husband, linking money owed to her father. Frank Stoneman had discovered this scheme and sensed that his long-lost daughter was in trouble. He sent his brother to investigate. Her Uncle Ned carefully evaluated both Marjory and Kenneth. He determined that Marjory was unaware of not only her husband's illegal activities but that much of it occurred during excessive drinking. Marjory was convinced; it was time to leave her husband and this short bizarre marriage. Her father was in Miami and had remarried. He sent money and a message for Marjory to come to Florida.

In September of 1915, at the age of twenty-five, Marjory boarded a train south, leaving behind her one-year-old marriage and her past to reunite with her father and create a new life. Frank Stoneman was the owner and editor of a start-up newspaper called the *Herald* in the "frontier" town of Miami. Frank and his wife, Lillius, welcomed Marjory with open arms, inviting her to live with them.

Frank Stoneman was known for the high standards of his newspaper. He investigated the accuracy of every fact that he printed. His strong opinions about Governor Napoleon Bonaparte Broward's intention to drain the Everglades were often reflected in his editorials. Marjory learned a great deal from her father in the first few weeks of their reunion.

After an apprenticeship filling in at her father's newspaper, Marjory was given the full-time position of society editor. Marjory's reporting connected her with events and people. Her writing led her to government officials, developers, and activists. Marjory often told about the time when she and Mary Jennings Bryan traveled to Tallahassee to lobby the Florida Senate to support the women's suffrage amendment. After telling about that trip and how the women kept their skirts away from the spittons, Marjory always joked and laughed about how persuasive she must have been because Florida was the last state to ratify the amendment.

While covering a story about a plumber's wife who was about to become the first woman in Florida to enlist in the Naval Reserve, Marjory decided it would be she who would join first. Her assignments with the government led her to work for the American Red Cross overseas.

Marjory returned to Miami from Europe in 1920 determined to live her life in her own way. She decided to write her own column and devote all her attention to exploring the geography of Florida. Holding a strong belief that a personal relationship would dominate her mind and her intentions, Marjory remained single for the rest of her life, enjoying the independence that a woman free from a husband and children gave her.

She was assigned the task, and her *Herald* column "The Gallery" was born. Added to this daily responsibility, she took over as assistant editor of the growing *Herald*. Marjory began to investigate and write more and more about the Everglades.

Marjory reacted physically to the stresses she was experiencing. The paper's publisher resented her criticisms of the development of Miami. She had taken on exposing and improving the horrible conditions in Miami's "Colored Town." In 1924, under the extreme stress of meeting newspaper deadlines, she—like her mother before—experienced a nervous breakdown. After rest and reevaluation, she decided she would change her literary goals and write differently. A successful career creating short stories was about to begin. The magazine business soared after World War I. She hired an agent from New York City and began freelance writing.

She wrote for magazines such as the *Saturday Evening Post* and the *Ladies Home Journal* for fifteen years eventually earning $1,200 per piece, an extraordinary amount for the 1920s and '30s. She wrote three plays and a great deal of poetry, but began to look to the possibility of becoming a novelist.

Her success as nationally recognized short-story writer gave her the financial independence to move out of her father's home. In 1926, at the age of 34, she contracted to build a functional home in Coconut Grove, an early settlement town outside of Miami that balanced gardens and wild Florida. She wanted a home that was sparse and more like a workshop. In the early twentieth century, Coconut Grove was the home to writers, painters, artists, and naturalists. Here she would live for the remainder of her life. Marjory danced, swam, and socialized—but never wanted to learn to drive a car.

She continued to suffer from nervous fatigue and emotional breakdowns. In 1941, Marjory's father died at the age of eighty-four. He had remained the editor in chief of the Miami *Herald* even though the Knight family had purchased the newspaper. Once again Marjory experienced a mental setback that required hospitalization. After she had healed, she felt that, at the age of fifty-one, she was entering a new beginning. A great release of energy seemed to launch her into her most ambitious and important project.

The epic Everglades book began with a publisher's request to write about the Miami River for a series on American rivers. Through the information she had gathered during her writing about this massive wetland, she was able to convince the publisher that the Everglades was actually a river—a river of grass. Viewing this vast area as a unique river rather than a swamp was an important step in the political battle to prevent the draining of this wetland. She held this viewpoint because of the slow flow of water from Okeechobee southward and the predominance of a sedge known as sawgrass. Marjory was determined to do the research and find the people who would help her develop this important lifework. In beginning this book and through its completion, Marjory began to feel the life and soul of this place. "There are no other Everglades in the world" are the famous words that open her book. "They are, they have always been, one of the unique regions of the earth; remote, never wholly known. Nothing anywhere else is like them."

Marjory was not an outdoorswoman. She did not camp, canoe, hunt, or fish. She told the Everglades poetic and powerful story through the land, its people, and its wildlife. It took her five years to complete and was released in 1947, coinciding with the founding of the Everglades National Park. Her book was an inspirational event even among naturalists.

In the 1950s, the U.S. Army Corps of Engineers rose to the top of Marjory's list of enemies of her beloved Everglades. In a major construction program, a complex system of canals, levees, dams, and pump stations was built to provide protection from seasonal flooding to former marshland now used for agriculture and real-estate development. Long before scientists became alarmed about the effects on the natural ecosystems of south Florida, Marjory Stoneman Douglas was railing at officials for destroying wetlands, eliminating sheetflow of water, and upsetting the natural cycles on which the entire system depends. Early on she recognized that the Everglades was a system that depended not only on the flow of water from Lake Okeechobee into the park, but also on the Kissimmee River, which feeds the lake.

In 1969, her Everglades book was twenty years old and Marjory was seventy-eight. As she approached her eighties, she would look to the next stage of her life: environmental activism and the great effort to save the Everglades. It was as if the Everglades had waited for her, and she was now ready to pour her passion into that fragile ecosystem. The crusade began with a grassroots attempt to prevent the building of a jetport in the Everglades and resulted in the organization known as Friends of the Everglades. Into her eighties and nineties, Marjory, blind but eloquent, would speak for the endangered panthers, Lake Okeechobee, the wood stork, the coral reefs, and the historic homes in Coconut Grove. Wearing her trademark floppy hat and thick glasses, she spoke at environmental conferences worldwide. In 1993, President Bill Clinton awarded her the Medal of Honor, calling her the "Mother of the Everglades."

Marjory Stoneman Douglas advocated taking care of yourself in your eighties so that you would be productive in your nineties.

When she was a few years from reaching her one-hundredth birthday, she sat with John Rothchild to record her life and her remarkable perspective on many subjects. Editing fifty cassette tapes, John gave the public the opportunity to discover this most remarkable woman in the book *Marjory Stoneman Douglas: Voice of the River*. In his introduction to her 1987 autobiography, he describes her appearance in 1973 at a public meeting in Everglades City: "Mrs. Douglas was half the size of her fellow speakers and she wore huge dark glasses, which along with the huge floppy hat made her look like Scarlet O'Hara as played by Igor Stravinsky. When she spoke, everybody stopped slapping [mosquitoes] and more or less came to order. She reminded us all of our responsibility to nature and I don't remember what else. Her voice had the sobering effect of a one-room schoolmarm's. The tone itself seemed to tame the rowdiest of the local stone crabbers, plus the developers, and the lawyers on both sides. I wonder if it didn't also intimidate the mosquitoes. ... The request for a Corps of Engineers permit was eventually turned down. This was no surprise to those of us who'd heard her speak."

On May 14, 1998, Marjory died peacefully in her home. Even at the end of her life, at age 108, she was working on yet another book, a biography of the nineteenth-century writer and environmentalist William Hudson, the author of *Green Mansions* and *Idle Days in Patagonia*. Although many of her friends believed her ritual evening cocktail was the secret to her longevity, Marjory maintained that having purpose in life kept her going for so long.

Her ashes were spread over the portion of the Everglades that bears her name. Marjory Stoneman Douglas was posthumously inducted into the National Women's Hall of Fame on October 7, 2000. Marjory continues to be remembered as Florida's Champion of the Environment.

Thank you Marjory, for showing us that regardless of one's age, we can speak for nature and make a difference.

Did you know?

Florida Everglades—A large marshland located in the southern portion of Florida. Though modified by agricultural development in central and southern Florida, the Everglades is the southern half of a large watershed originating in the vicinity of Orlando known as the Kissimmee River. The Kissimmee flows south and discharges into Lake Okeechobee, a very large (730 mile), shallow (10 feet) freshwater lake. Water leaving Lake Okeechobee in the wet season creates the Everglades.

Women's Suffrage Movement—Refers to an economic and political reform movement aimed at extending suffrage—the right to vote—to women. Universal women's suffrage did not come until the Nineteenth Amendment to the U.S. Constitution was ratified in 1920.

U.S. Army Corp of Engineers—A federal agency made up civilian and military personnel. The Corps' mission is to provide engineering services to the United States.

Explore the Land that Influenced Marjory Stoneman Douglas

Everglades National Park

In south Florida, this national park preserves the portion of the Everglades south of the Tamiami Trail, but represents on 27.3 percent of the original area. The park covers 2.3 million acres and is a World Heritage Site.

Web Site: www.nps.gov/ever

References and Recommended Readings

River of Grass, 1947, revised edition 1988, by Marjory Stoneman Douglas.

Road to the Sun, *1952*, Marjory Stoneman Douglas.

Freedom River, 1953, by Marjory Stoneman Douglas.

Hurricane, 1958, by Marjory Stoneman Douglas.

Alligator Crossing, 1959, by Marjory Stoneman Douglas.

Florida: The Long Frontier, 1967, by Marjory Stoneman Douglas.

Marjory Stoneman Douglas: Voice of the River, 1987, Marjory Stoneman Douglas with John Rothchild.

Marjory Stoneman Douglas, Guardian of the Glades, 2002, Kieran Doherty.

The Wide Brim: Early Poems and Ponderings of Marjory Stoneman Douglas, 2002 by Jack Emerson Davis.

Zora Neale Hurston

January 7, 1891 (Nostasulga, Alabama)–January 28, 1960 (Fort Pierce, Florida)

Mama exhorted her children at every opportunity to "jump at de sun." We might not land on the sun, but at least we would get off the ground.

Zora Neale Hurston

Zora Neale Hurston was a novelist, folklorist, and anthropologist whose fictional and factual accounts of black heritage are unparalleled. Her autobiography, *Dust Tracks on a Road*, begins with the words "I have memories within that came out of the materials that went to make me. Time and place have had their say." Zora's "place" was the frontier wilderness of Florida. She grew up in Eatonville, the only incorporated all-black town in America. Playing in the pine barrens and oak scrub, she unconsciously absorbed impressions about the wild flora and fauna. The memory of these sights, smells, and sounds inspired her curiosity and creativity.

Zora explored and understood all parts of her home state of Florida. She traveled its every mile gathering folktales. *Mules and Men*, a collection of Hurston's folklore from Florida, is rich in the magic of the natural world. The lyrical descriptions of settings, the realistic dialogue, and the haunting simplicity of symbols demonstrate her knowledge of real Florida. Zora sometimes characterizes the people of an area by the plants and animals around them. Regional plants and animals not only lend authenticity to settings and dialogue, they also provide a central symbol for each of her three Florida-based novels. *Jonah's Gourd Vine* is filled with snake imagery. In *Their Eyes Were Watching God*, often considered her finest literary achievement, the central symbol is a pear tree. A large mulberry tree is the main image in *Seraph on the Suwannee*. In *Their Eyes Were Watching God*, Zora also includes the most calamitous natural disaster in modern Florida history: the drowning of more than two thousand people on the south shore of Lake Okeechobee during the devastating 1928 hurricane.

Zora was a strong, vigorous, confident woman. Her fierce independence both as a person and as a writer can be traced to her frontier roots. At the time of Zora's birth, just before the turn of the century, central Florida was reeling from the Great Freezes of 1893–94, which devastated the citrus industry and sent many immigrants fleeing north. About the same time, it was discovered that the seemingly barren Florida sands were laden with phosphate. Some of the rowdiest mining towns in the American frontier replaced those blighted communities of former northerners. The already existing sawmill and turpentine camps were as notorious in their lawlessness as the mining boomtowns. This era provided rich and colorful backdrops to many of Zora's stories. She sought to know this life intimately as she did her research alone, traveling and sleeping in her Model T, pistol at her side.

Zora grew up in a community of black people who respected their ability to govern themselves. Her own father had written the Eatonville town laws. He sent her to a private school in Jacksonville. Her mother, who died when Zora was thirteen, encouraged her to "jump at the sun." This community affirmed its right to exist and loved her as an extension of itself.

The world-renowned writer Alice Walker, who early in her career committed herself to Zora's work, states, "Zora was a woman who wrote and spoke her mind—as far as one could tell, practically always." At a time when it was believed that "real" black writers should concentrate on the struggle with the white majority, Zora focused on themes of self-discovery and African American culture, which her contemporaries did not hold in high regard. She believed "the oldest human longing" is for "self revelation." Zora's work achieved limited success during her lifetime as her theme was not taken seriously. More than sixty years later, one sees in Zora's writings black women characters who struggle to liberate themselves in a world dominated by men and their values. Political content existed in her work, though at the time gender issues were invisible.

Zora also had an air of mystery; for example, she gave birthdates of 1898 through 1903. Evidence shows she was born January 15, 1891. Her autobiography leaves much unanswered. She began her higher education at Howard University but left after a few years, unable to support herself. Later she was offered a scholarship to Barnard College, where she received her B.A. in anthropology working with fellow student Margaret Mead in her research. Zora lived in New York at the crest of the Harlem Renaissance and was an assistant to the popular novelist Fannie Hurst. Her numerous marriages were short. She disappeared for extended periods of time.

Zora was most productive in her written work in the '30s and '40s and frequently returned to Florida. She applied her ethnographic training to document African American folklore in her critically acclaimed books. Zora joined the Federal Writers' Project for the state of Florida. Strongly supported by Eleanor Roosevelt, the Writer's Project was the New Deal's answer to literary unemployment. A unit of the WPA, the project began in 1935 to provide jobs for hundreds of authors unable to practice their craft in the Depression economy. Zora became an editor for the Florida project in April of 1938, working independently and often mysteriously.

Zora was awarded a Guggenheim Fellowship to travel to Haiti and conduct research on conjure in 1937. Her work was significant because she was able to break into the secret societies and expose their use of drugs to create the Vodun trance. Zora's work slid into obscurity for decades for both cultural and political reasons.

Many readers objected to the representation of African American dialect in Zora's novels. Her stylistic choices in terms of dialogue were influenced by her academic experiences. Thinking like a folklorist, she strove to represent speech patterns of the period, which she documented through ethnographic research. For example (Amy from the opening of *Jonah's Gourd Vine*):

> "Dat's a big ole resurrection lie, Ned. Uh slew-foot, drag-leg lie at dat, and Ah dare yuh tuh hit me too. You know Ahm uh fightin' dawg and mah hide is worth money. Hit me if you dare! Ah'll wash yo' tub uh ' gator guts and dat quick."

Some of her contemporary critics felt that Zora's decision to render language in this way caricatured black culture. In more recent times, however, critics have praised Zora for her artful capture of the actual spoken idiom of the day. During her research, Zora visited places no other anthropologist thought to go. She went to country churches, bootleg joints, and the turpentine camps. She posed as a bootlegger's girlfriend from Jacksonville "waiting for her man to get out of the joint."

Some of these amazing descriptions had been stored unpublished in the Library of Congress until Kristy Anderson, an independent filmmaker, discovered them. Turning the material over to the Huston estate in 1991, the work was published in 2001 as *Every Tongue Got to Confess: Negro Folk-tales From the Gulf States*. In addition, ten unpublished plays were also discovered at the Library of Congress as the layers of Zora's life continue to unfold.

In 1948, an incident sent Zora back to Florida for good. A ten-year-old boy accused her of sexual molestation. Zora was in Honduras on a research trip at the time of the supposed offense, and the charge was eventually dismissed. But the incident damaged her reputation and in great part prevented further publishing prospects. Coming back to the Florida she loved helped her regain her energy.

Her characteristic restlessness was replaced with a need for peace and the feeling of being home. The natural world of Florida provided this for her. At the age of sixty (as always passing for much younger), Zora finally settled down in a one-room cottage. Although penniless, being able to garden, write, and care for her pets gave her a feeling of being alive and happy. Zora wrote to a friend that "Living the kind of life for which I was made, strenuous and close to the soil, I am happier than I have been for at least ten years." Her love of Florida is reflected in another letter north she wrote in the winter of 1950 while on board a boat: "And God keeps His appointment with Miami every sundown. Berthed on the east of Biscayne Bay, I can look to the western side, which I never fail to come top-side and do around sunset. Thus I get the benefit of His slashing paint brush all the way. It is just too marvelous. The show is changed every day, but every performance is superb."

Zora spent her last ten years as a freelance writer for magazines and newspapers. Her life ended in poverty and obscurity, although she remained gallant and unbowed until the end. She worked in a library in Cape Canaveral, Florida, and as a substitute teacher in Fort Pierce. Zora opposed the Supreme Court ruling in the *Brown v. Board of Education* case of 1954; she felt the physical closeness of blacks to whites was not going to be the salvation her people hoped for, as she herself had had many experiences to the contrary. She worried about the demise of black schools and black teachers as a way to pass on cultural tradition to future generations of African Americans. Zora voiced this opposition in a letter, *Court Order Can't Make the Races Mix,* which was published in the *Orlando Sentinel* in August 1955.

Zora Neale Hurston died of a stroke on January 28, 1960, in a welfare nursing home in Fort Pierce, Florida; she was estranged from family and friends.

In 1973, African American novelist Alice Walker (years before her *The Color Purple* was written) and literary scholar Charlotte Hunt traveled to Fort Pierce to find this "bodacious" woman's grave. On locating the segregated cemetery called the Garden of Heavenly Rest, they discovered that Zora's unmarked grave was in a field of weeds. Before leaving the town, Alice Walker purchased a gravestone to place in her honor that stated "Zora Neale Hurston,

'Genius of the South.'" The actual location of Zora's body is still unknown.

The publication of Alice Walker's article "In Search of Zora Neale Hurston" in the March 1975 issue of *Ms. Magazine* revived interest in her work and helped spark a Hurston renaissance. Few American writers have experienced as dramatic a change from obscurity to worldwide acclaim. Zora Neale Hurston is now one of the most widely read and studied American authors. More than a million copies of her 1937 novel *Their Eyes Were Watching God* are in print.

Zora's friend Marjorie Kinnan Rawlings once wrote that she was proud of her blood and her people, and many would add "and of her land." Zora's writings show that she recognized the intense wild beauty of the Florida countryside and how it shaped those who lived close to the land.

Thank you, Zora, for showing us the strength of women through the strength of nature.

Did you know?

Pine Barrens—Pine barrens are plant communities that occur on dry, acidic, infertile soils dominated by grasses, low shrubs, and scattered pine trees.

Alice Walker—American author and feminist. She received the Pulitzer Prize for Fiction in 1983 for her critically acclaimed novel *The Color Purple.*

Margaret Mead—An American cultural anthropologist.

Vodun—Word for spirit. Voodoo in Haiti is highly influenced by Central African traditions.

Conjure—Casting spells.

WPA—President Franklin D. Roosevelt established the Works Progress Administration on May 6, 1935, as the centerpiece of his New Deal. This program was designed to employ as many workers as possible and not to distribute the money as handouts.

Explore the Land that Influenced Zora Neale Hurston

Eatonville, Florida

Located six miles north of Orlando, Eatonville was the first all-black town to be incorporated after the Emancipation Proclamation of 1863.

Web Site: www.zoranealehurston.com

References and Recommended Readings

Sweat, 1926, by Zora Neale Hurston.

How It Feels to Be Colored Me, 1928, by Zora Neale Hurston.

The Gilded Six-Bits, 1933, by Zora Neale Hurston.

Jonah's Gourd Vine, 1934, by Zora Neale Hurston.

Mules and Men, 1935, by Zora Neale Hurston.

Tell My Horse, 1937, by Zora Neale Hurston.

Their Eyes Were Watching God, 1937, by Zora Neale Hurston.

Moses, Man of the Mountain, 1939, by Zora Neale Hurston

Dust Tracks on a Road, 1942, by Zora Neale Hurston

Seraph on the Suwanee, 1948, by Zora Neale Hurston

Zora Neale Hurston, A Literary Biography, 1980, Robert E. Hemenway.

Zora Neale Hurston, a Life in Letters, 2002, collected and edited by Carla Kaplan.

"In Search of Zora Neale Hurston," *Ms. Magazine,* March 1975, by Alice Walker.

Wrapped in Rainbows: The Life of Zora Neale Hurston, Valerie Boyd.

Every Tongue Got to Confess: Negro Folk-tales From the Gulf States, 2001, by Zora Neale Hurston

Myrtle Scharrer Betz

February 22, 1895 (Scharrer's Island, Florida)–January 2, 1992 (Dunedin, Florida)

Like a loosely strung necklace, they
lie off shore along the coast·
Their age can be told by
the growth they contain·
As one barrier is being worn down,
another is forming outside of it·

Myrtle Scharrer Betz

Myrtle Scharrer Betz was born February 22, 1895, on a barrier island off the coast of west central Florida. A body of land designed by nature to hold back the storms that raged from the Gulf of Mexico. Myrtle was raised by a remarkable father who taught her to be self-reliant. These lessons created a life in harmony with the land, the sea, and all creatures on what is now known as Caladesi Island State Park.

Myrtle's father, Henry Scharrer, arrived in New York City from Switzerland in 1883. At the age of twenty-three, he traveled to Wisconsin to help Swiss dairy farmers duplicate the quality of the cheese of their homeland. After offering his advice, he planned to travel throughout the United States and to return to Switzerland using the money he had deposited in a bank on his arrival. Henry discovered that the bank had failed, and the money for his passage home lost.

For five years he found work on farms and ranches throughout the Midwest, eventually reaching San Francisco. Henry then journeyed back across the country to New Orleans. There he caught a ship to the port of Tampa to find employment and plan his continuing adventure. South America was to be his next stop, a place he envisioned to be paradise. He prepared to explore the southern continent before returning to Switzerland. As he helped build the Plant Hotel, now the University of Tampa, he used his earnings to buy and outfit the sailboat that would take him on his venture.

While sailing the local waters in his new purchase, a sudden storm caused him to shelter his vessel, *Anna*, in a barrier island bayou off the Gulf of Mexico. Grounded for the night, Henry awoke to explore a wilderness of beach scrub, pine flatwoods, and oak hammock. It was April, the height of the spring migration. Henry discovered he was sharing this refuge with hundreds of birds of varying colors and shapes. A deer appeared, and a gopher tortoise scurried into its burrow. The mullet were so thick that Henry was able to stun one with an oar for his island meal. Without plotting a course, he had stumbled onto paradise. He had found the place he wanted to call home.

Henry became a U.S. citizen to obtain a land patent through homesteading. This remarkable adventurer was soon to become the owner of 157 acres on a land mass known as Hog Island. Many homesteaders abandoned living on their land at the end of the five-year requirement and their ownership was secure. Henry worked his acreage to create a home. He proved to be such a caretaker of his property that soon his slice of paradise was nicknamed Scharrer's Island. This immigrant understood how to live off the land.

Henry sold his extra produce and honey door to door in the village of Dunedin. Once again, he was guided to his destiny. He fell in love with an Irish companion to one of his customers, the Malone family. On a moonlit island night in April of 1894, Henry Scharrer married Catherine McNally. When the festivities ended, they stood in front of their island home listening to the music of their seaside wilderness. A paradise would now be shared.

On February 22, 1895, in their island board and batten home, Catherine gave birth to a little girl. An indigo bunting seeking shelter from the winter storm occurring on that day perched on Catherine's bed to welcome this child into the world. The baby was named Myrtle after the plant with fragrant berries used to make aromatic candles. The wax myrtle thrived on their island as did the child namesake. Myrtle grew to love nature. Wildlife was her friend and companion. The seashore treasures were her storybook. She was taught to embrace a sustainable lifestyle, to protect and carefully harvest the resources of the land and sea around her. The Scharrer family practiced methods of fishing and gathering shellfish that would sustain the supply, striving to live in harmony with their island environment.

When Myrtle was seven years old, Henry rowed both Catherine and his daughter to the mainland to seek medical attention for his progressively ailing wife. The return trip was heavy with grief. Catherine died as a doctor tried to save her life. The depth of this man and child's loss was magnified by the discovery that vandals had ransacked their home. Catherine's trunk was missing, and with it the only picture Henry and Myrtle had of her. In spite of this devastation, Henry decided that he would continue to raise his only child on the island. Myrtle was taught to fish, handle a boat, throw a mullet net, navigate, use tools, trap, plant a garden, harvest crops … and shoot a gun.

On Sundays, Myrtle and her hardworking father rested from the island chores. This pioneer child would comb the beach as if turning the pages of a book. Stories of wonder grew from the constantly changing wave-washed island shoreline. Her own fairy tales emerged from the pearl oyster, cracked bottle, and mysterious broken oars. Myrtle's enjoyment came from the companionship of her dog and her rich observations of simple incidents: a brilliant sunset, a flock of roseate spoonbills, their eagle neighbors playing games with the osprey, the sounds that emerged as daylight changed to night. A favorite place was the twin pine that reminded her of a lyre. Listening to the sounds of wind and earth's creatures, she could hear music.

Henry taught his daughter to read and write, but soon Myrtle begged to attend a formal school. At the age of nine, Henry considered Myrtle sturdy enough to row the two-mile distance to the town of Dunedin to attend her classes. She kept a smile to herself as a new teacher introduced a physical fitness program of arm swings and torso bends, not surprising since this little girl had been up since 3:00 a.m. helping her father with a large catch of fish before rowing St. Joseph's Sound against a northeast wind.

For fifteen years, Myrtle banded birds for the Bureau of Biological Survey, recording the migrants as well as the island's residents. She became skilled at navigating and fishing the local waters. Myrtle learned to balance the population of raccoons by trapping during the winter months, earning a personal allowance in her youth and extra family money in her adult life. Myrtle saw much beauty, but she also endured great heartache through her experience of the senseless destruction of wildlife, habitat, and her own personal property. Henry's philosophy was radical for his time. He protected wildlife and habitat in an era when breeding herons and egrets were slaughtered for their plumes and burrowing owls were clubbed on the shore to use as fish bait. Bald eagles were regularly shot for fear they would carry off livestock. Vegetation was burned or cut for any reason. Myrtle witnessed the horror of dolphins slaughtered because they were perceived as competitors for fish.

Henry Scharrer was an independent, educated foreigner and a champion of his way of life. He was not always popular with some of the local people of the area, but many sought his favor to participate on his well-known island tours, visiting their resident bald eagle nest and hearing the embellished tales of Indian lore. Travelers to the area, such as Carl Sandburg and Eddie Rickenbacker, sought out and regularly visited this amazing man and his daughter on their island homestead.

The dynamics of Florida weather governed the pattern of many of their days. It was also the backdrop for some of their most extraordinary experiences. Myrtle and her father encountered dramatic storms, learning to read the clouds, the wind, and the behavior of wildlife. Henry rode out the big storm of October 1921 with merely a yard to clean up and a few shingles to replace. Quite an event, considering this was the storm that split Hog Island in half. Erosion widened the cut, creating Hurricane Pass into the Gulf of Mexico. The southern portion would eventually be known as Caladesi. The island to the north would be called Honeymoon.

Like most young people, Myrtle grew restless. She worked for a time at the famous Belleview Biltmore Hotel in Belleair. There she met a man from New Jersey seeking a life in Florida. After visiting Scharrer's Island, Herman Betz stayed in touch with Myrtle and then wrote to Henry asking for his daughter's hand in marriage. Myrtle convinced herself that perhaps it was time to share this life with a husband.

After marrying in September of 1914, they moved to Miami. A small house in a strange town shared with a man she hardly knew now replaced her previous life. After two years, Henry encouraged Herman and Myrtle to move back to the Dunedin area. They settled in St. Petersburg. After the 1921 hurricane, they returned to Myrtle's island paradise. They built their home next to Henry's on the southeast portion of the island.

Myrtle did not desire jewels or fine clothes. She longed for a horse. Prince was purchased with a monetary gift from her father when the circumstances of the Depression made this creature available for sale. One of Myrtle's most vivid memories was riding her treasured horse to the beach to watch a waterspout forming offshore in the Gulf of Mexico. She and Prince stopped within 100 feet of the column of wind and water and watched as it met the shore, marched inland, hit a sabal palm, and dispersed into a low cloud.

Myrtle and Herman became fishing partners to earn their income. Myrtle recalls that those years fishing together were the happiest of their fifty-five-year marriage. In the early '20s it was rare to see a woman make her living from the sea. Often when Myrtle caught kingfish alone she overheard many conversations floating across the water discussing the "woman in the boat." Myrtle's commercial fishing days ended with the birth of their baby girl, Marion, in 1928. She showered her little daughter with all the treasures of living in this paradise. Soon Myrtle began thinking about the difficult decision to move to the mainland so her daughter might attend school and avoid the rigors of commuting by boat.

In June of 1934, the Betz family moved from the island to the mainland, leaving much that Myrtle loved. She was able to move her horse, Prince, rowing him on a barge! Her new home sat on a lot in Dunedin, 50 x 100 feet. Promising her father regular visits, she traveled to Scharrer's Island as often as she could, especially as his health began to fail. After the evening meal, carrying her oars on her shoulders, Myrtle would hurry to the waterfront where she kept an eighteen-foot skiff. The journey across the sound gave her the peaceful time to once again be absorbed by nature. Often the moon shining through the pines onto the water created a pathway into her father's bayou. The touch of the salty night air on her skin combined with the intensity of fragrance reminded Myrtle of what touched her soul.

On one visit she saw how ill her father had become, and decided it time to bring Henry to her home. Henry was such a notable in town that this move made the front page of the local paper. A few days later, Myrtle was able to row back to the island to retrieve some items for her father. She discovered that her father's home had been vandalized again, this time taking Henry's violin, much of his radio collection, and the silver watch his father had given him as a boy. Myrtle vowed her father would never know of this outrage. On Myrtle's later visits, the house continued to be stripped, and eventually it was burned. Henry died on Christmas day in 1934. He turned his face west as if looking toward his island home for the last time, sighed, and closed his eyes. He was eighty-four.

From the mainland, Myrtle made an impact as she wrote for magazines and newspapers, flavoring her words with the essence of her remarkable life. Her knowledge of the natural world gained from acute observation made her writing vivid. The strength and independence essential to her island survival gave her the wisdom to make a difference. On her father's death, Myrtle inherited the island homestead and in 1946 sold the 157 acres for $50,000. She had the vision to place a restriction in the deed that it was to remain a wildlife refuge and no alterations could be made unless approved by the Audubon Society and the local Marine Science Center, a clause that still exists in the management plan of Caladesi Island State Park.

Myrtle Scharrer Betz lived a life that was truly remarkable, and at the age of eighty-seven she was encouraged to record her memories in a book she titled *Yesteryear I Lived in Paradise—The Story of Caladesi Island*. Written in a notebook without editing, her words captured the spirit of life on Scharrer's Island at a time when the pioneer era was ending. She died in January of 1992, just before her ninety-seventh birthday. Her ashes are sprinkled in the Gulf of Mexico, near the place of her birth on her beloved island. Today her granddaughter, Terry Fortner, keeps Myrtle's memory alive through remarkable community presentations remembering the little girl who grew up on a paradise island in what is now the most densely populated county in Florida.

Thank you Myrtle, for inspiring us to honor the land and her creatures and to love Caladesi Island.

Did you know?

Gopher Tortoise—The gopher tortoise averages ten inches in length and weighs nine pounds. It is protected as a threatened species. It burrows into the ground with many adaptations for digging. It is considered a keystone species, one in which many other species depend for survival. Over 200 species of animals are dependent on the gopher tortoise burrow for safety.

Homesteading—In the United States, the Homestead Act (1862) allowed anyone to claim up to 160 acres of land. After clearing and working the land for five years, the homesteader would receive title to the land from the government.

Wax Myrtle—Also known as Southern bayberry or candleberry because early American colonists used the fruit's pale blue waxy covering to make fragrant bayberry candles. The tree's distinctive, fragrant scent comes from volatile oils contained in tiny glands on the leaves.

Mullet—A variety of schooling fish found throughout the world, but the black or striped mullet is prevalent in the southern United States. Sometimes referred to as the "jumping mullet," this is the primary mullet found in Florida, both in Gulf of Mexico and Atlantic waters. Mullet range up to thirty inches in length and have an average weight of three to six pounds.

Barrier Islands—Sometimes called barrier spits, are found on coastlines all over the world, but are most noticeable along the East Coast of North America, where they extend from New England down the Atlantic Coast, around the Gulf of Mexico and south to Mexico. Barrier islands are fragile, constantly changing ecosystems that are important for coastal geology and ecology.

Mangroves—Three species of mangroves are found in Florida: the red mangrove, black mangrove, and white mangrove. They have been protected since the 1970s. Typically, red mangroves grow along the water's edge, black mangroves grow on slightly higher elevations than the red mangroves, and white mangroves grow upland from the red and black. Mangroves grow in saltwater and in areas frequently flooded by saltwater. Mangroves provide protected habitat, breeding grounds, and nursery areas to many land and marine animals. Mangroves also provide shoreline protection from wind, waves, and erosion.

Oak Hammock—Hardwood hammocks are localized, thick stands of hardwood trees that can grow on natural rises of only a few inches of land. In south Florida, hammocks occur in marshes, pinelands, and mangrove swamps. Hammocks may contain many species of trees, including the sabal palm, live oak, red maple, mahogany, gumbo limbo, and cocoplum. Many types of epiphytes ("air plants") and ferns can be found here as well.

Sabal Palm—Also known as Cabbage Palm, is Florida's state tree.

Irish Lyre—The lyre is a stringed musical instrument. The lyre was ordinarily played by plucking with a plectrum, like a harp.

Carl Sandburg—An American poet, historian, novelist, and folklorist.

Eddie Rickenbacker—Best known as a World War I hero and Medal of Honor recipient.

Explore the Land that Influenced Myrtle Scharrer Betz

Caladesi Island and Honeymoon State Parks

Barrier Island State Parks located on the Gulf of Mexico across St. Joseph's Sound from Dunedin, Florida, north of Clearwater Beach.

Web Site: www.nps.gov/ever

Reference

Yesteryear I Lived in Paradise—The Story of Caladesi Island, 1984, 1991, Myrtle Scharrer Betz. 2007 edition enlarged by Terry Fortner.

Marjorie Kinnan Rawlings

August 8, 1896 (Washington, D.C.)–December 14, 1953 (St. Augustine, Florida)

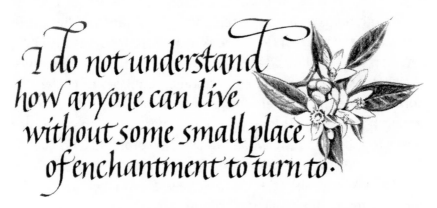

I do not understand how anyone can live without some small place of enchantment to turn to.

Marjorie Kinnan Rawlings

Marjorie Kinnan (pronounced kin-NAN) Rawling's creative energy blossomed when she discovered the harmony of place. This northern-born woman found her authentic literary voice after she bought and began to farm an orange grove near Cross Creek, Florida. Her classics include the Pulitzer Prize–winning novel *The Yearling* and her autobiographical *Cross Creek*. Marjorie Kinnan Rawlings writes "When I came to the Creek, and knew the old grove and farmhouse at once as home, there was some terror, such as one feels in first recognition of a human love, for the joining of person to place, as of person to person, is a commitment to shared sorrow, even as to shared joy."

From 1926 to 1928, Marjorie wrote "Songs of the Housewife," a daily feature that started modestly in the Rochester (New York) *Times-Union*, but was soon syndicated in fifty newspapers. She was the first newspaper column writer to celebrate the housewife, even though she did not glory in the role herself. In this series, readers heard the voice of an emerging feminist that courageously insisted that women be respected.

Marjorie arrived to Florida wilderness when she was thirty-two. She lived the first half of her life in northern cities. Born in Washington, D.C., in August of 1896, she went to college at the University of Wisconsin to study English. Marjorie married fellow student Charles (Chuck) Rawlings and moved to New York. Looking for something to revive their personal and professional lives, they traveled to the town of Cross Creek in 1928. Named because it lay between the Lochloosa Lake and the Orange Lake, Marjorie was fascinated with its remoteness, wildness, simplicity of life, and its Florida Crackers. It was here she felt a sense of place—the peace of finding home. Marjorie returned north to attend to the transition of moving to the South, while Chuck's two brothers who lived in central Florida found a citrus farm for them to purchase. With the goal to make one last attempt to write successful fiction, she also hoped to rescue their failing marriage.

Marjorie fell in love with the Florida countryside, and almost immediately her writing began to flourish. Many novelists focus on people and the relations of human character; Marjorie was stirred by place. She looked at people as they related to the land and was convinced that this relationship was as important as any relationship between people. Like Thoreau, she felt the life in plants, the spirit of a river or of a great storm. She felt that it would be difficult to find happiness until you found a place with which your spirit could live in harmony with your surroundings. Marjorie, found her soul mate in Cross Creek.

Unable to repair the turmoil of their life together, Marjorie divorced Charles five years after moving to Cross Creek.

Marjorie was unique in having the insider's commitment of love for her subject, but also the outsider's objectivity. Marjorie's literary world comprised the rural portions of three counties in north central Florida: Alachua, Putnam, and Marion. This area is part of a region where the northern temperate zone passes into the semitropics, so it contains trees, shrubs, and flowers of both zones. The raising of citrus, given such prominence in her writing, reflects the northernmost commercial groves in the state.

Like other Yankee newcomers, Marjorie was continually amazed at the lavishness of the natural beauty that surrounded her and began to write these impressions in the form of a journal. From the beginning, she immersed herself in learning about every plant, shrub, tree, and flower. She cooked three meals a day on a wood-burning stove and washed clothes in an iron pot. Wary at first, the neighbor Crackers soon warmed, sharing their lives and experiences. Marjorie faced the problem of how to reflect in her writing honestly about the evolution of Southern society without the racism that existed in the language of her new friends. She was especially amazed by the harmony in which her neighbors lived in their wild environment.

On the first day of hunting season, Marjorie found herself lost in the scrub. Here she encountered the palpability of silence. Reflecting on this experience, she later expressed that she felt no fear even though she was definitely lost and alone. She sat on a log and simply waited. In the quiet of her solitude she discovered an all-encompassing peace deeper than anything she had ever known. She sensed that such an area with its wildness and its silence must have a pronounced effect on the character of people who lived there.

In 1930 Marjorie sold a short story entitled "Cracker Chidlings" to *Scribner's* magazine. It appeared in the February 1931 issue, catching the attention of chief editor Maxwell Perkins. The editor wrote Marjorie asking if she had ever thought about writing a novel. Her enthusiastic response revealed that she was "vibrating with material like a hive of bees in swarm." The thoroughness with which she attempted to understand cracker life is illustrated by her trek into the Big Scrub to live for two and a half months in late summer of 1931. She made arrangements to stay with the Fiddia family—a ninety-pound white-haired wisp of a woman who still plowed her own field behind a mule, and her son Leonard, master woodsman, hunter, trapper, fisherman, and purveyor of moonshine.

In the early 1930s, as she contemplated this world of the "Crackers," Marjorie felt that she had actually discovered a door through which she could step back in time. She realized that living in the simplicity of nature gave her a clarity that filled her with illumination and excitement. The texture of this land was running through her veins. Within two years of her arrival in Florida, she had peered deeply into this lost world and set down in substance the outlines of her most important books and stories.

After writing *South Moon Under* in 1933 and *Golden Apples* in 1935, Marjorie opened the world of the Big Scrub to generations with *The Yearling* in 1938. This timeless story of the tender relationship of a young boy and his tame fawn has been translated into thirteen languages and made into a motion picture starring Gregory Peck and Jane Wyman. Her autobiographical *Cross Creek* went to print in 1942 and captured the public's curiosity as had *The Yearling*.

Marjorie married again in 1941. Her second husband, Norton Baskin, was a hotelier and businessman from St. Augustine. She divided her time between her new home with Norton and Cross Creek. Marjorie was a hardworking determined woman. Equally comfortable with the Crackers as she was with the professors she socialized with at the University of Florida, she did not fit into the mold of an educated woman of the '40s and '50s. She loved to entertain, cooking seasonally with her homegrown herbs and vegetables. Her *Cross Creek Cookery* was published the same year as her cherished *Cross Creek*.

Marjorie had a reputation for volatility, hard drinking, and reckless driving. She was also known for her generosity and advocacy of civil rights. She adored her pets. Her circle of friends included Ernest Hemingway, Thomas Wolfe, Robert Frost, and Margaret Mitchell. Her understanding of human rights came from her friendships with Zora Neale Hurston, Mary McLeod Bethune, and Indira Gandhi.

Despite her literary success, she was prone to moods of depression and drunken fits while smoking five packs of cigarettes a day. Adding to her personal turmoil was a slander lawsuit brought against her by Zelma Cason, one of the neighbors she wrote about in *Cross Creek*. It was the first such lawsuit brought against an author for depiction of character in a book. The case went to trial in Gainesville in 1946 for invasion of privacy. The impact of this five-year ordeal kept her from ever writing again about the place that had brought her back to life. She lost the case, as well as her spirit. She spent more and more time away from Cross Creek, staying at her other home, The Cottage, in Crescent Beach, just south of St. Augustine.

It took Marjorie ten years to complete her next book, *The Sojourner*, which was set in the North. In order to absorb the natural backdrop so vital to her writing, she bought an old farmhouse in New York and spent part of each year there. *The Sojourner* was finally published in 1953. In December of that year, she died suddenly of a cerebral hemorrhage at the age of fifty-seven.

Marjorie is buried in Antioch Cemetery, a short distance from Cross Creek. Her husband, Norton, became the "keeper of her flame." Laboring over what to put on her gravestone, Baskin decided on: "Marjorie Kinnan Rawlings 1896–1953, Wife of Norton Baskin. Through Her Writings She Endeared Herself to the People of the World." Norton Baskin survived her by forty-four years, passing away in 1997. They are buried side by side.

As a pioneer environmentalist, an independent woman, and a supporter of civil rights at a time when few white Southerners were willing to take that stand, Rawlings's reputation has outlived those of many of her contemporaries. A posthumously published children's book, *The Secret River,* won a Newbery in 1956. Movies were made, long after her death, of her story "Gal Young 'Un" and her semi-fictionalized memoir *Cross Creek* (Norton Baskin, then in his eighties, made a cameo appearance in the latter movie).

Marjorie bequeathed most of her property to the University of Florida. She envisioned a place where students could come and stay. She wanted it to be a place of resources and inspiration. In 1970, the Florida Parks Service began managing the site. Staff are responsible for the garden, grove, house, animal care, visitor services, special school tours, and general housekeeping tasks. August and September are spent on cleaning absolutely everything, painting, maintenance, and other archival duties. Major restoration was completed by 1996, the year of Marjorie Kinnan Rawlings's one-hundredth birthday. The Parks Service threw a party in celebration. Each year the first Sunday in August finds an open-to-the-public birthday bash that draws hundreds.

Marjorie Kinnan Rawlings felt the magic and mystery that the tropics tend to arouse in people born in colder climates. This Yankee wrote her books with a continuous sense of wonder at the rich natural beauty with which she was surrounded. She wrote of nature less as a scientist and more as a person determined to communicate personal experience. Scientific accuracy was seamlessly woven into her story. Marjorie wrote intimately of her sense of oneness with other living things and continuously sought to discover human relevance in objects and events in nature. Nature was for her a place of beauty and harmony, a restorative source of health. Marjorie believed humankind was born with an attachment to the earth that led to her conviction that the closer one's intimacy with the natural world, the fuller and happier would be one's life.

Marjorie felt she would leave little impact on this world because she had never had children. She ends *Cross Creek* by giving her philosophy of the land and our connection to it.

> But what of the land? It seems to me that the earth may be borrowed but not bought. It may be used, but not owned. It gives itself in response to love and tending, offers its seasonal flowering and fruiting. But we are tenants and not possessors, lovers and not masters. Cross Creek belongs to the wind and the rain, to the sun and the seasons, to the cosmic secrecy of seed, and beyond all, to time.

Thank you Marjorie, for helping us to understand the magic of connecting to place. For some of us it is the shoreline and for others the mountains, but we must find what speaks to our soul to feel complete.

Did you know?

Crackers—Name given to native residents of Florida whose ancestors drove herds of cattle to various shipping points in Florida. Long cowhide whips were used that "cracked" so loudly they could be heard for miles.

Big Scrub—Name for Ocala National Forest.

Thoreau—An American author, naturalist, and philosopher who is best know for *Walden*, a reflection on simple living in natural surroundings, and his essay *Civil Disobedience*, an argument for individual resistance to civil government in moral opposition to an unjust state.

Cason vs. Baskin—By definition, libel is a malicious publication or a defamatory writing. Zelma Cason sued Marjorie Kinnan Rawlings for defamation of character because of a passage in *Cross Creek*.

Explore the Land that Influenced Marjorie Kinnan Rawlings

Cross Creek Historic State Park

Marjorie Kinnan Rawlings Historic State Park is located between Ocala and Gainesville in Cross Creek, at 18700 S. CR 325 in north central Florida.

Web Site: www.floridastateparks.org/marjoriekinnanrawlings

Ocala National Forest

This forest covers approximately 607 square miles in central Florida. It is located three miles east of Ocala, Florida, sixteen miles southeast of Gainesville. Established in 1908, the Ocala National Forest is the oldest national forest east of the Mississippi River and the southernmost national forest in the continental United States. The word "Ocala" is thought to be a derivative of a Timucuan Indian term meaning fair land or big hammock.

Web Site: www.stateparks.com/ocala.html

Reference and Recommended Reading

South Moon Under, 1933, by Marjorie Kinnan Rawlings.

Golden Apples, 1935, by Marjorie Kinnan Rawlings.

The Yearling, 1938, by Marjorie Kinnan Rawlings.

When the Whippoorwill, 1940, by Marjorie Kinnan Rawlings.

Cross Creek, 1942, by Marjorie Kinnan Rawlings.

Cross Creek Cookery, 1942, by Marjorie Kinnan Rawlings.

The Sojourner, 1953, by Marjorie Kinnan Rawlings.

The Secret River, 1955, by Marjorie Kinnan Rawlings.

The Marjorie Rawlings Reader, 1956, by Marjorie Kinnan Rawlings.

Frontier Eden: The Literary Career of Marjorie Kinnan Rawlings, 1966, Gordon Bigelow.

Invasion of Privacy: The Cross Creek Trial of Marjorie Kinnan Rawlings, 1988, Patricia Nassif Acton.

Marjorie Kinnan Rawlings: Sojourner at Cross Creek, 1990, Elizabeth Silverthorne.

Idella, Marjorie Rawlings' "Perfect Maid," 1992, Idella Parker.

The Creek, 1993, J. T. Glisson.

Cross Creek Kitchens, 1993, Sally Morrison and Kate Barnes.

Short Stories by Marjorie Kinnan Rawlings, 1994, edited by Roger Tarr.

Poems by Marjorie Kinnan Rawlings, Songs of a Housewife, 1996, edited by Roger Tarr.

Marjorie Kinnan Rawlings and the Florida Crackers, 1995, Sandra Wallus Sammons and Nina McGuire.

Anne Morrow Lindbergh

June 22, 1906 (Englewood, New Jersey)–February 7, 2001 (Passumpsic, Vermont)

o PATIENCE, patience, patience, is what the sea teaches. One should lie open, empty, choiceless as a beach, waiting for a gift from the sea.

Anne Morrow Lindbergh

Anne Morrow Lindbergh's life was filled with adventure, success, and heartbreak. The wife of aviator Charles Lindbergh was talented in her own right. One of her enduring accomplishments was creating the insightful *Gift from the Sea*. First published in 1955, it remains in print, a treasured gift for women of all ages. Anne wrote this book while exploring the incredible shoreline of Captiva Island, Florida. Choosing to vacation alone at a beach house shortly after the death of her mother, Anne sought to explore the need to achieve a simple, uncluttered life in a world of complex change. Already famous for her remarkable journals, she sought to discover her own identity within the boundaries of a complex marriage. Anne's ability to connect her soul's longing with the intricate beauty of this beach and its creatures is a gift for generations.

Anne Spencer Morrow was born into a New Jersey family of wealth, education, and prestige on June 22, 1906. The second of Dwight and Elizabeth Morrow's four children, Anne was raised in a household that fostered achievement. Her father's career encompassed lawyer, partner at J. P. Morgan & Co., U.S. Ambassador to Mexico, and senator from New Jersey. Her mother was active in women's education, serving on the board of trustees and briefly as acting president of her alma mater, Smith College. Anne also attended Smith College, graduating in 1928.

When Charles Lindbergh returned to the United States after making his historic solo flight from New York to Paris, he was a hero and a celebrity. In the weeks and months that followed, Lindbergh received over 100,000 telegrams and cables of congratulations and adulation from citizens of all walks of life. In December 1927, Lindbergh accepted the invitation of Dwight Morrow, then the American ambassador to Mexico, to visit the Latin American country. Lindbergh flew to Mexico, covering 2,100 miles in poor weather conditions. Over 150,000 people greeted him on his arrival in Mexico City.

Nearly lost within that crowd was the one person who caught Lindbergh's eye, the ambassador's twenty-one-year-old daughter, Anne. Lindbergh was drawn to Anne's quiet and contemplative nature. Yet within the spirit of this budding young poet was an adventurous woman eager to seek out new worlds. Falling in love gave her the confidence to do just that. "The man I was to marry believed in me and what I could do, and consequently I found I could do more than I realized," she later recounted in her diaries. As their courtship progressed, Lindbergh taught Anne how to fly. The two were married in a brief, simple ceremony at the Morrow's estate in Englewood, New Jersey, on May 27, 1929. Anne was twenty-three years old. That same year, she also flew solo for the first time.

In the 1930s, Anne and Charles together explored and charted air routes between continents. When Charles became fascinated by the possibilities of aerial photography, Anne steadied their open-cockpit Curtiss Falcon biplane as he took hundreds of photographs in his search for ancient cliff-dweller ruins in the American Southwest. During his travels in the Yucatan, he had seen what appeared to be a Mayan city. Anne returned with him and three other men to photograph the ruin in the Central American wilderness. It was an arduous expedition with many hours of low flying over wild and treacherous terrain. Anne did more than her share of the work and was exhilarated by the experience made possible by her husband's faith in her abilities and courage.

At Charles's insistence, Anne made her first trip in a glider. After one day of instruction, while several months pregnant, she became the first woman in the United States to be issued a first-class glider pilot's license. While seven months pregnant, Anne helped Lindbergh break the transcontinental speed record on Easter morning in 1930. They flew through storms with Anne sick and in pain. Upon landing they were swarmed by reporters. Charles rebuffed them and only then did Anne allow herself to be taken out of the cockpit on a stretcher for fear her illness would overshadow Charles's accomplishment in the media reports.

On June 22, 1930, on her twenty-fourth birthday, Anne gave birth to a son, Charles Augustus Lindbergh, III. Like his father after his historic flight, Charlie Jr. immediately became a celebrity.

Anne began flying with her husband one month after giving birth. Being alone with Charles in a plane thrilled her as much as it had the first time she had flown with him. Charles Lindbergh was a college dropout with little appreciation for the arts; he preferred practical jokes. When they were in a plane, the vast difference in their personalities, class, and education vanished. Flying at his side, she witnessed the aviation pioneer who was courageously exploring the atmosphere, breaking records, and making archeological discoveries while passionately loving the earth and sky. Anne acquired the knowledge to operate a high-frequency radio set, studied around-the-world flight navigation, and how to transmit and receive Morse code. She became Charles's copilot, radio operator, and navigator as they flew to China via

Canada and Alaska to open a new path to the Orient for commercial air travel. Later she eloquently described this experience in her first book, *North to the Orient*. It was on this flight that she received the supreme compliment bestowed by her husband: when questioned about taking his wife on such a dangerous flight, Charles said, "You must remember that she is crew."

Anne Morrow Lindbergh's interest in flight was not a hobby. In 1934, the National Geographic Society awarded her its Hubbard Gold Medal for her accomplishments in 40,000 miles of exploratory flying over five continents with her husband. In addition, she was awarded the Cross of Honor of the U.S. Flag Association in recognition of her accomplishments in surveying transatlantic air routes. She learned to fly a Bird biplane and received her pilot's license in May 1931 becoming the first licensed female glider pilot in the United States.

With adventure came tragedy. Charles and Anne endured constant publicity from the press. Household help were offered bribes for information about their private lives. On a bleak, windy evening on the first of March in 1932, their little boy, twenty-month-old Charlie Jr., was kidnapped. He was taken from their New Jersey home outside of Hopewell while Anne and Charles prepared for bed. After a massive investigation, the baby's body was discovered four miles from the Lindbergh's home.

Even after the famous Lindbergh kidnapping trial and the birth of their second child, they were haunted by a frenzied press and continued threats. The Lindberghs decided on a self-imposed exile in England and later to the small island of Iliec off the coast of France. While in Europe, Anne and Charles advocated isolationist views that led to their fall from grace in the eyes of many Americans.

Not one to embrace organized religion, Anne preferred to find solace, peace, and inspiration in nature. The sky, the sea, the wind, and the stars were the sources of her creativity. Her best writing reflects this deep communication with the natural world. Anne shared Charles's intense concern for ecology and conservation. In 1940, while in her fourth pregnancy, she flew a five-day trip with her husband to explore the then unspoiled Everglades. In 1970, at her alma mater Smith College, she argued, "human values spring from earth values and must be supported by them."

With her mother's death, Anne's struggle focused on what she "must be for Charles … and what I must be for myself." In an effort to resolve this conflict, she began to explore its ramifications in prose. In an effort to find a retreat from the distractions and responsibilities of both Charles and their five children, she rented a beach house on Captiva Island to be alone.

Gift from the Sea contains eight written meditations on different seashells, seeing them as symbols for various aspects of life and relationships. Anne advocated that a woman occasionally take time from her responsibilities to nourish herself spiritually, startling advice for the chauvinistic era of the mid-'50s. Ironically, Anne's editors feared the book had no chance for commercial success. They tried to persuade her to change the title to *The Mass of Men Lead Lives of Quiet Desperation*, a suggestion she wisely vetoed. *Gift from the Sea* was to become Anne Morrow Lindbergh's most successful and enduring work. Accused of being a Nazi propagandist fifteen years earlier, *Gift from the Sea* immediately reestablished Ann's reputation as a popular and beloved woman author. Thousands of American women immediately identified with the problems and concerns voiced in her inspirational essays. Her use of natural imagery and the singular narrative voice establishes a simplicity that accomplishes empathy and intimacy between reader and narrator. The metaphor provided by the seashells subtly expresses her social concerns. The simplicity she achieves is the deceptive result of a disciplined and controlled literary style. Her eye for detail remains evident throughout.

She later edited and published five volumes of her diaries covering the period between 1922 and 1944. Over the course of their forty-five-year marriage, Charles and Anne lived in New Jersey, New York, Maine, Michigan, Connecticut, Hawaii, England, and Switzerland. Charles died on Maui in 1974. It is reported that from 1957 until his death, Charles had an affair with a Bavarian woman twenty-four years younger than he, whom he supported financially. One of the woman's children came to suspect that Lindbergh was their father and made her suspicions public after finding among her mother's effects snapshots of and letters from Charles. The affair was kept secret, and only in 2003, after the passing of Anne and the mistress, did DNA testing prove that Charles had fathered his mistress's three children.

After suffering a series of strokes in the early 1990s, Anne continued to live in her home in Connecticut with the assistance of round-the-clock care. In 1999, Anne went to live near her youngest daughter, Reeve, and her family in a small home built on Reeve's Vermont farm. Anne died in 2001 at the age of ninety-four. Reeve Lindbergh's book *No More Words* tells the story of her mother's last years. In Reeve's introduction to the fiftieth anniversary edition of *Gift From the Sea*, she reflected on her mother:

> Her book offers its readers, finally an extraordinary kind of freedom, and I think this is the reason it continues to be so well loved, and so well read, after all these years. I am talking about the freedom that comes when one chooses to remain open, as my

mother did again and again, to life itself, whatever it may bring: joys, sorrows, triumphs, failures, suffering, comfort, and above all, always, change.

At whatever point one opens *Gift From The Sea*, to any chapter or page, the author's words offer a chance to breathe and to live more slowly. The book makes it possible to quiet down and rest in the present, no matter what the circumstances may be. Just to read it—a little of it or in its entirety—is to exist for a while in a different and more peaceful tempo.

Anne Morrow Lindbergh, along with her husband, shared a commitment of finding a balance between nature and technology. Her insights guide those of us who continue that quest for balance.

Thank you Anne Morrow Lindbergh, for your courage and your appreciation of the natural world ….. and for the gift of sharing your insights with us.

Did you know?

Seashell—The shell of a saltwater mollusk. A typical mollusk has a soft body protected by a shell. The shell is formed by a layer of tissue called the mantle. Most mollusks belong to one of four main groups: gastropods (whelk), bivalves, cephalopods, and chitons.

Glider—An aircraft that flies without an engine.

Mayan—Relating to an ancient civilization of Central America.

Isolationism—A belief that political rulers should avoid entangling alliances with other nations and all wars not related to direct territorial self-defense.

Explore the Land that Influenced Anne Morrow Lindbergh

Captiva Island, Florida

Located in southwest Florida, north of Naples offshore in the Gulf of Mexico—A barrier island that originally was part of Sanibel Island.

Web Site: www.captivaisland.com

References and Suggested Readings

www.lindberghfoundation.org

North to the Orient, 1935, by Anne Morrow Lindbergh.

Listen! The Wind, 1938, by Anne Morrow Lindbergh.

The Wave of the Future, 1940, by Anne Morrow Lindbergh.

The Steep Ascent, 1944, by Anne Morrow Lindbergh.

Gift From the Sea, 1955, by Anne Morrow Lindbergh.

The Unicorn and Other Poems, 1956, by Anne Morrow Lindbergh.

Dearly Beloved, 1962, by Anne Morrow Lindbergh.

Earth, 1972, by Anne Morrow Lindbergh.

Bring Me a Unicorn, 1972, by Anne Morrow Lindbergh.

Hour of Gold, Hour of Lead, 1973, by Anne Morrow Lindbergh.

Locked Rooms and Open Doors, 1974, by Anne Morrow Lindbergh.

The Flower and the Nettle, 1976, by Anne Morrow Lindbergh.

War Within and Without, 1980, by Anne Morrow Lindbergh.

A Gift for Life, 1992, Anne Morrow Lindbergh and Dorothy Herrmann.

Anne Morrow Lindbergh: Her Life, 1999, Susan Hertog.

No More Words, 2001, by Reeve Lindbergh.

Return to the Sea, 2005, Anne M. Johnson.

Anne Morrow Lindbergh: First Lady of the Air, 2006, Kathleen C. Winters.

Jacqueline Cochran

May 11, 1906 (Muscogee, Florida)–August 9, 1980 (Indio, California)

Adventure is a state of mind—and spirit.

Jackie Cochran

Jackie Cochran was raised on the sawdust roads of Florida in the early 1900s. Soaring out of poverty, she became one of the greatest women pilots in aviation history. At the time of her death in 1980, she held more speed, altitude, and distance records than any other pilot—male or female.

The towering longleaf pine forests of north Florida drew Jackie's eyes to the sky. Old-growth trees ranging from 100 to 300 years old climbed 120 feet into the atmosphere. Jackie and her family lived in the impoverished conditions of rural northwest Florida. Their difficult lives were a sharp contrast to the monetary value of the longleaf pine that surrounded them with beauty. Countries emerging from the devastation of World War I desired this solid insect-resistant hardwood for construction. Virgin forests of trees with branches forming miles of continuous green canopy were coveted for their precious lumber. The longleaf pine meant gold for the handful of men who owned the land and the equipment to start the lumber mills and turpentine stills. After the turpentine had been drained from the live pines and the trees were felled, debarked, cut, planed, dried, and shipped out as lumber, the mills would close and move to the next forest. Young Jackie's playground was once the largest continuous forest on the North American continent. Where 90 million acres existed, less than 10,000 acres of old-growth longleaf pine forests remain today.

Jackie's father and two brothers worked in these sawmills. The so-called sawdust roads connected the many mill towns that sprang up in the panhandle of Florida. The low areas next to the bodies of water needed to transport the logs often became marshy and flooded. A mule and wagon carted around leftover chips and sawdust to spread over the dirt road keeping them passable when it rained, thereby creating the sawdust roads of Florida. When the mill closed, the family scrambled for work and a new place to live. Dozens of busy towns with names like Sampson, Millville, Bagdad, Panama City, Paxton, and Defuniak Springs appeared in northwest Florida. These abandoned communities would often slide into economic decay and sometimes just disappear, later to be known as a sawmill ghost town with only a cemetery to mark its existence.

Jackie's family moved many times, but the mill town always looked the same to her. Shacks surrounded the sawmill along with a company store or commissary and a doctor. The doctor was busiest in the mill towns that featured the two-sided band saws with twice the opportunity of being maimed or killed. Jackie's father had a standard wage deduction of fifty cents a month to have the necessary medical care to patch up workers and keep the mill running. The millworkers were paid in chips instead of money. These chips were only good in the commissary and to pay rent on the issued housing. With average pay about one dollar a day, it was a powerful way to keep the employees and their families enslaved to the mill. As long as the logs kept coming in, the saws keep turning. Everyone did something to support the wealth of the mill owners. When traveling to the next town by train, Jackie would jump out at stops to gather the knotty parts of the pine trees that could not be sawed but were full of tar for burning in the train engine furnaces. This helped pay the family's passage to their next home.

Jackie absorbed the mission of the mills that shaped her day-to-day life. As the workers destroyed beautiful forests, slashing and searing the pines back to stumps, she knew it was a terrible way to live … and to do business. Jackie was independent and defiant even in her youth. She stayed in those woods many nights hoping to run away with gypsies or the circus who visited the mill towns. On a lonely, dark night returning home at the age of six, she heard wailing coming from the foot bridge she was about to cross. Her friends had warned her of the ghost who lived in the cemetery. Something rose up and stretched long arms toward her. Running toward the sounds rather than away, she found a calf with its leg stuck in a wooden bridge. Her realization of the true nature of what she feared stayed with her as she faced unimaginable risks later in her life.

Jackie's first experience with height came thirty feet up in a tree. She was captivated by the festive life the area black families had after their workday. While dancing and singing, these neighbors were unaware of a little white girl perched outside the second-floor window. Night after night little Jackie got close to the stars and took in another way of life. She knew even then that the physical horizon she saw was limited only by her imagination. One evening after falling asleep on her limb, she fell the thirty-foot distance to the ground. No bones were broken, but she would recall this memory at more dizzying altitudes.

By 1920 almost all of the old-growth pine had been cut, sawed into lumber, and shipped out on the railroads. Of her sawmill life Jackie said, "If you want someone to really enjoy the pleasures of heaven … just pitch her into hell for a spell. Perhaps that's why I enjoyed my life to the brimful." She described herself as a "refugee from sawdust road."

Resisting the structure of school, Jackie never quite made it through second grade. The only scholarly nurturing came from Miss Bostwick, the northern teacher in town. In Jackie's young eyes, this beautiful woman not only inspired her to imagine what she could become but paid her a wage to chop and stack firewood, an early start to her dreams and her physical strength.

Throughout Jackie's life as an aviator-celebrity, she claimed to be an orphan raised by a foster family with two sisters and two brothers. Uncertain of her date of birth, she guessed May 11 somewhere between 1905 and 1908. Jackie described selecting her last name randomly from a phone book in Pensacola in her twenties as she ventured out in her new life. In 1999, Jackie's niece Billie Pittman Ayers published an account of what she claims is her aunt's authentic beginning. Regardless of why Jackie's early life history differs from her family's disclosure, something gave this woman an incredible drive.

At the age of eight, Jackie broke away from the declining sawmill life by working with her family in a Georgia cotton mill. At fourteen, she entered another world as a helper in a Georgia beauty parlor. She learned an exciting trade as she practiced using hair dye on the "fancy ladies" or prostitutes who came in the back door. Her knowledge of how to operate the new permanent wave machines opened the door to travel. Earning enough to buy a Model T, she also became an expert at keeping the engine tuned.

Encouraged to leave the beauty profession for nursing, Jackie returned to Florida to become a medical assistant to a country doctor who cared for sawdust road families. Unable to live in the conditions of her roots again, she headed for the nearest big town. In Pensacola, she returned to the business of beauty by becoming a partner in a shop. While taking a break to attend beauty school in Philadelphia, Jackie was approached to teach. Here she realized there was more she could do with her talent. She sold her share in the Florida beauty shop and moved to New York City, where she got a job with Antoine in the Saks Fifth Avenue salon. Following her well-to-do clients to their Miami winter retreats, a chance invitation to a party furthered the distance from her poverty-stricken past: she met her future husband, millionaire Floyd Odlum.

Perhaps Jackie's interest in flight was tapped by attending dances at the Pensacola Naval Flying School. In 1932, at the age of twenty-six, Jackie decided to take a six-week vacation and do something with her mind. Despite her lack of formal schooling, Jackie was bright. She wanted to learn how to fly and obtain her pilot's license. Her new friend, Floyd, had bet her the $495 class instruction fee she could not do it in that six-week time. Despite the frivolousness of the bet, her desire was real. After three weeks of instruction at Roosevelt Field on Long Island, she obtained her pilot's license in a Fleet trainer with a sixty-horsepower engine. She had won the bet, but had also decided on her future: Jackie wanted to become a professional pilot. The next year she enrolled in the Ryan Flying School in San Diego.

At that time, the Air Force did not exist, and the Army Air Corp or the Navy had a few basic planes. Hot pilots and good planes were to be seen and flown in circuses. Now Jackie had a real opportunity to run away with a circus. Jackie joined the Johnny Livingston Air Circus in New York to learn the skills she knew she would need to advance her opportunities. She prepared for the MacRobertson London to Australia Race. In the early days of aviation, these races were about more than winning the prize money. They were often the only way airplane designers and manufacturers could show their innovations. Winners might walk away with cash, but the airplane maker wanted to walk away with orders for more planes. The MacRobertson race was the first flying project in which manufacturers took an interest in Jackie's flying. This race was a promotional opportunity for Sir MacPherson Robertson, the maker of Old Gold candy. The proposed route stretched over 11,300 miles and followed a course crossing deserts, mountains, tropical rain forests, water of all kind, and distance. Jackie and her copilot, Wesley Smith, did not complete the race, but the experience and exposure continued to drive this amazing woman toward new barriers.

Not only was Jackie researching her next step toward learning about aviation, she was exploring the idea of creating her own beauty products. Flying at high altitudes and over long distances encouraged her to create a moisturizer to solve the problems she was having with her own skin. In 1935, Jacqueline Cochran

Cosmetics was born. She was in the competitive circle of Helena Rubenstein, Dorothy Gray, and Elizabeth Arden—the women who founded the cosmetic industry in the '30s. She even designed the lipstick and gloss that Marilyn Monroe used for the movie *Gentlemen Prefer Blondes.*

Jackie always made sure she had a feminine appearance, holding up reporters while she applied her lipstick before exiting her cockpit. People were amazed at how small she seemed until they noticed the steel poise of her body. She did not use nail polish in an attempt to draw attention away from her strong masculine hands. She preferred the company of men. Yet Jackie dedicated her business life to making it easier for women to feel good about themselves. By 1934, she had her commercial pilot's license and used this angle to fly to her accounts and market her products.

Her objective of every flight was to go faster or further through the atmosphere. A competitive nature drove her to fly higher than anyone else and to bring back new information about the plane, its engine, the fuel, an instrument, the air, or the pilot herself. Besides establishing records, she enabled airplane manufacturers to insist on cabin pressurization as well as mandatory use of oxygen masks above certain altitudes. Jackie was the driving force behind the pursuit of aviation medicine. In addition to her racing, Jackie was a test pilot. In the early years of aviation, this was a dangerous, nerve-racking experience. Jackie's ability to see, hear, and read all her senses came from a childhood that taught her to handle whatever came her way.

Jackie married Floyd Odum after his divorce on May 11, 1936. Floyd was fourteen years older than Jackie. He was a self-made millionaire by the age of thirty. Floyd was intensely devoted to Jackie and encouraged not only her aviation career but her desire to break records. Floyd and Jackie fell in love with the desert of Indio, California, and built their dream ranch as their base as they each pursued individual and joint ambitions.

Women pilots in the '30s were a special breed. Jackie and Amelia Earhart were close friends. The outside world saw them as competitors, but in reality, Amelia was to distance what Jackie was to speed. Their mutual interests extended into the curiosity of the psychic phenomena and ESP. As Amelia prepared for her solo flight around the world, Jackie practiced locating her on practice flights through sensory instinct. On that tragic July day in 1937, Jackie heard Amelia's cry for help through powerful internal messages.

She tried unsuccessfully to guide the rescue mission. Unable to save her beloved friend, she never again called on her sixth-sense sensitivities. She felt that Amelia had handed her the torch to carry on to the next aviation goal for women.

A pilot's ears and eyes are crucial. Jackie's remarkable ability to use her senses helped her become the first woman to make a blind landing. In March of 1939, Jackie established a women's national altitude record. That September she broke the international open-class speed record for men and women while finding time to win the New York to Miami Air Race. Her understanding of the human body and flight enabled her to push aviation medicine into recognized existence and made sure that there was money and attention to nurture it into maturity.

Jackie used her flying skills in a display of remarkable patriotism. She became the first woman to pilot a bomber across the North Atlantic and organized a group of twenty-five American women to fly for Great Britain in the war effort. In 1943 she was appointed to the general staff of the U.S. Army Air Forces and directed all phases of Women's Air Force Service Pilots (WASP) program. Her wisdom and experience attracted many notable people into her circle. Connections and persistence enabled her to successfully lobby for a separate air force after World War II. She was close friends with both Dwight D. Eisenhower and Lyndon Johnson. She even drew the attention of Howard Hughes, who rented her plane when she would not sell to him.

On May 21, 1953, at the age of forty-seven, under the guidance of Chuck Yeager who first broke Mach 1, Jackie entered a Canadian-built Sabre Jet F-86 and became the first woman to exceed the sound barrier. As Jackie piloted her plane away from earth, she saw daylight fade even though it was noon. The stars came out. She was eight and a half miles above ground. Initiating the split "S" maneuver, she began the almost vertical full acceleration dive back toward earth. Her eyes left the noontime stars, and fixed on the Mach meter. Relaying her readings to Chuck, who was flying another plane, she felt the physical violence of approaching the speed of sound and the incredible calm as she entered that moment in history. Jackie wanted to achieve surpassing Mach 1 for both emotional and spiritual reasons.

Whenever Jackie sought to regain perspective on her place in this universe, she went out to her desert ranch lawn and peered through her telescope into the solar system. She was captivated by the ability to see the light of not just the moon but of stars perhaps not in existence at that moment. Although not able to actively participate herself, she saw the need for women to be present at the birth of the aerospace industry and was instrumental in presenting the data that women were as capable as men for space travel.

On August 9, 1980, Jackie Cochran died at her home in Indio, California. Throughout her life Jackie was asked to give talks or write about adventure. Being the first woman to break the sound barrier was the greatest thrill of her life. Her passion is evident in the quote "Pity the man or woman who doesn't have the chance to love the way I loved flying." Although she certainly had found adventure in flying, world travel, and business, Jackie also saw adventure in the simple aspects of the natural world around her.

Thank you Jackie, for showing us that a woman can rise above any obstacle and courageously explore the wonders of nature.

Did you know?

Longleaf Pine—The longleaf pine is native to the southeast United States, found along the coastal plain from eastern Texas to southeast Virginia and extending into northern and central Florida. These forests were the source of naval stores—resin, turpentine, and timber—needed by merchants and the navy for their ships.

Turpentine—A fluid obtained by the distillation of a oil-like resin primarily obtained from pine trees.

Mach—The ratio of the speed of the body to the speed of sound in the surrounding medium.

Explore the Land that Influenced Jackie Cochran

The Red Hill Region

Home to some of the last remnants of the great longleaf pine forests remaining in the nation. The soil is red clay from the Appalachian Mountains deposited during the last Ice Age. The Red Hills region is a unique 300,000-acre area of the southeastern United States overlapping parts of southwestern Georgia and north Florida, north of Tallahassee.

Web Site: www.heartoftheearth.org

References and Suggested Reading

www.wingsacrossamerica.us/wasp/jacqueline_cochran.htm

The Stars at Noon, 1954, by Jacqueline Cochran.

Jackie Cochran, 1987, by Jacqueline Cochran and Maryann Bucknum.

Jacqueline Cochran: America's Fearless Aviator, 1997, Nina McGuire and Sandra Wallus Sammons.

A WASP Among Eagles, 2000, by Ann Baumgartner Carl.

Superwoman Jacqueline Cochran, 2001, by Billie Pittman Ayers and Beth Dees.

Rachel Carson

May 27, 1907 (Springdale, Pennsylvania)–April 14, 1964 (Silver Spring, Maryland)

Those who contemplate the beauty of the earth find reserves of strength that will endure as long as life lasts.

Rachel Carson

Rachel Carson, the remarkable writer and scientist, explored the shores of Florida when she wrote *The Edge of the Sea* in 1955. In this book Rachel aimed, in her own words, "to take the seashore out of the category of scenery and make it come alive—an ecological concept will dominate the book." She studied the marine life from the rocky coast of Maine to the sandy shores of the Atlantic coastal plain, south to the "mangrove ghost forests" bordering the Florida coast. During her research in Florida, she delighted in exploring the floor of the ocean near Key West using primitive diving equipment. Due to poor weather conditions, Rachel experienced a short one-time opportunity to view the undersea world. That instant gave her a lifetime memory from which to write her impressions of the sea in both *The Edge of the Sea* and her earlier book *The Sea Around Us*.

Rachel Carson began the process of writing *Silent Spring* in 1958. This book evolved from her belief that all living things are connected to their environment. *Silent Spring* changed the course of history. It was *The Uncle Tom's Cabin* of modern times. Published in 1962, Rachel's message was an indisputable warning of the danger of pesticides, especially DDT. She exposed publicly for the first time the facts that link modern contaminants to all parts of the environment. Her focus was the long-lasting chlorinated hydrocarbon insecticides. These chemicals move through the environment and being fat soluble, are stored in animal tissue and recycled through food chains. *Silent Spring* prompted the federal government to take action against water and air pollution, as well as against pesticides, years before it otherwise would have done anything.

Rachel Carson's intense feeling of interconnection with the natural world was ahead of her time. The term "environment" had little meaning, and the concept of ecology was unknown. This unique awareness was at the core of everything she wrote. Through her personal exploration as a child and adult, she was witness to the mystery and wonder of all life. Rachael understood the thread that connects all living things both scientifically and with her soul.

Rachel was born on May 27, 1907, outside the Allegheny River town of Springdale, Pennsylvania. As a child she explored the woods around her family's home with long walks often with her mother, Maria. Rachel acquired a deep spiritual appreciation of the beauty and mystery of the natural world. Rachel's acuity of observation and eye for detail were shaped during these childhood explorations. Although Rachel grew up far from the coastline, she was strongly attracted to the great oceans she had never seen. When she entered the Pennsylvania College for Women, today known as Chatham College, it was with the intention of becoming a writer. But in her sophomore year, she found her passion in natural history and the sciences. This young student felt that her destiny was somehow linked to the sea.

Rachel went on to Johns Hopkins University to get her degree in zoology and later to the Marine Biological Laboratory at Woods Hole, Massachusetts, where she saw the sea for the first time. In addition to teaching at Johns Hopkins and the University of Maryland in the mid-'30s, Rachel worked for the United States Bureau of Fisheries (which later became part of the Fish and Wildlife Service). Despite her schedule, she never quite gave up the desire to write. She once said, "Eventually it dawned on me that by becoming a biologist, I had given myself something to write about."

Late in 1941, her first book, *Under the Sea-Wind*, was published. Her unusual style of writing captured the cycles of seasons and the struggle of each creature to survive. Her voice was that of a scientist and poet describing the wonder of all she discovered in nature. In *Under the Sea-Wind,* Rachel sought to convey an intimate portrait of the sea and shore creatures. Her writing creates a world of air and water for the reader to enter. The three parts of the book focus on different protagonists, the sea birds, the mackerel, and the eel, linking them together through their dependence on the sea. But literary success was delayed; one week after her book was published, the Japanese attacked Pearl Harbor and America's attention turned to fighting a global war.

Rachel spent the war years in her government office in Washington D.C., and for a short time in Chicago. At thirty-six, she was a respected government science writer and editor. Just as the world was entering transition, Rachel felt the restlessness of walking just short of her life's purpose. Rachel became the editor in chief of the Fish and Wildlife publications. As Rachel continued to advance in the government with the responsibilities that accompanied, so did the load she carried personally. After her father died, her mother, Maria, came to live with her and eventually took on the position of being Rachel's house manager and creative confidant—a place in Rachel's life that Maria would hold firmly until the day she died. Rachel also had financial responsibility for her sister, Marion, and her sister's two children.

After the war, Rachel proposed a series of twelve booklets for the general public featuring the national wildlife refuge system. She was approved to begin *Conservation in Action*. This project provided a challenge to expand her research and creativity. Rachel had a vision to explore the natural refuges throughout the United States. While traveling, she remained in contact with the wildlife biologists in the Fish and Wildlife divisions. She was aware of the alarm some biologists felt toward the use of the new synthetic pesticide dichlorodiphenyl-trichloroethane, known as DDT, and how it would affect fish and wildlife. DDT was used by the military against lice and insect-borne diseases during the war. Its effectiveness as an insect repellent was well established, but the chemical screening for its safety to humans had barely begun.

Rachel also stayed informed of the Red Tide invasion of the Gulf Coast of Florida. In 1946, south Florida fishermen reported fish kills where the water had turned red. By December of 1947, millions of fish had died. As an information specialist, Rachel compiled data about this phenomenon from many sources and wrote an article that was published by *Field and Stream*, titled "Killer from the Sea." Ironically this article was accompanied by a picture of an emergency crew spraying the dead fish that littered the Florida beaches with a mixture of DDT and deodorant to control flies.

Rachel was discovering the emotional and physical costs of having a public career during the day and a private writing career at night. This, coupled with being the head of a household, may have caused a series of hospital stays between 1945 and 1948. Whatever she coped with, Rachel continued to organize the information she had collected about the oceans with plans to expand it into a book.

In 1948, Rachel decided to look for a literary agent to help her with her next publishing venture. It was this process that led her to Marie Rodell. Rachel and Marie complemented each other. These two women developed a strong working relationship that allowed Rachel to focus more on her research and creativity and less on finding a publishing house for her work.

In 1951, first as a series in the *New Yorker* then as a best seller, her book *The Sea Around Us* became a literary sensation. She brought the natural history of the earth's oceans into everyone's grasp. As acclaimed as her work was by both the scientific and academic communities, many male readers were reluctant to admit that a woman could deal with a scientific subject of such complexity. The sexism Rachel encountered was blatant—from critiquing her appearance to speculation on the true gender of the author. Nevertheless, as the publisher struggled to meet the demand, Rachel was contemplating the next step on her journey.

While on leave from her job researching the Florida Keys for a seashore guide, Rachel decided it was time to retire from her government work. In May of 1952, she filled out her resignation form in Key West and forwarded it to Washington, D.C. The release of her impending governmental responsibilities may have given Rachel clarity to conceive of her next book. As she sorted through the information on the Florida Keys, she realized the shoreline was really divided into three types: rock, sand, and coral. She had found the creative energy for a companion volume to *The Sea Around Us*.

The Atlantic Coast represented the environment of rocky shore life dominated by tides, sandy shores ruled by waves, and ocean currents determining life along southern coasts. This shoreline concept was common to shores all over the earth. In addition to her creative freedom, Rachel's success allowed her to truly become part of her beloved shoreline. She bought a strip of land in the Boothbay Harbor area on the Maine coast in 1953 and built a cottage she called Silverledges, which became her second home.

It was here that Rachel met and bonded with her neighbors Dorothy and Stanley Freeman. Rachel and Dorothy discovered in each other an intense love of nature, as well as a mutual devotion to their pet cats. Their friendship and love for each other would guide and comfort them for the remainder of their lives.

The Edge of the Sea was published in 1955 and quickly became a tremendous success. Rachel's third book rose rapidly on the *New York Times'* best-seller list to number two, just behind Anne Morrow Lindbergh's *Gift from the Sea*.

Rachel's niece Marjie had gone into hiding with Rachel's emotional and financial support to give birth to an out of wedlock son, Roger. Although Rachel now supported another family member, she loved sharing the wonders of the sea and shore with her nephew. After *The Edge of the Sea*, Rachel began writing *Help Your Child to Wonder*. This project reflected Rachel's ability to help others feel rather than just know nature through wonder and awe.

Another Florida connection developed when Rachel met W. Curtis Bok. Through their mutual interest in conservation, Rachel became involved in the Bok family's philanthropic preservation project of the Singing Tower in Lake Wales, Florida.

After a prolonged illness, Rachel's niece died in 1957 at the age of thirty-one. Now at the age of fifty and at the peak of her literary career, Rachel took on the daunting responsibility of adopting her five-year-old great-nephew, Roger, in addition to the constant care of her eighty-eight-year-old mother.

As Rachel's interest in conservation increased, she grew troubled by how casually chemicals were poured into the environment. The justifications offered by both industry and government for the unrestricted use were weak and without validity. It was apparent that the new chemicals posed a major threat to much of the natural world. What ultimate effect this massive chemical barrage would exert on human life itself, no one seemed to know. She saw clearly that man was, more than ever before, approaching the earth not with humility, but with arrogance.

Fuel was added to Rachel Carson's concern in 1958 as word spread of the USDA's Fire Ant Program in the South, including Florida. This insect had reached the United States apparently from South America soon after World War I. It had spread gradually through most of the southern states without causing an undue amount of alarm. Then, in 1957, the USDA launched a massive propaganda campaign using press releases, newspaper articles, and motion pictures against the fire ant. It followed up its verbal barrage with a deadly application of dieldrin and heptachlor, two of the most potent chlorinated hydrocarbon insecticides, in a campaign to eradicate the fire ant. In this pursuit, vast sums of money were wasted and great numbers of wild creatures were poisoned—not to mention the unknown harm to humans. Few seemed to evaluate the effects of aerial spraying as citizens wiped the poison off their picnic tables in Florida parks. But two women in Long Island, New York, sought to protect their organic garden from this onslaught through a lawsuit against the government. Their effort captured Rachel's attention.

The four-year task of writing *Silent Spring* began with a letter from a close friend of Rachel's in New England. Olga Owens Huckins owned a bird sanctuary. According to Olga's letter, the sanctuary had been sprayed unmercifully by the government. Her friend asked Rachel to use her influence with government authorities to begin an investigation into pesticide use. Rachel decided it would be more effective to raise the issue in a popular magazine; however, publishers were uninterested. Even in the emptiness that followed the death of her mother in 1958, Rachel was clear on her mission. She had found her next book.

Rachel began an exhaustive journey of uncovering data that was often suppressed. She was aware of the USDA's desire to expand its influence and leadership in American agriculture through the application of science and technology. Pesticide use was one of the most visible and important results. Rachel knew that she had to remain low key about her project. She is quoted "I am pressing ahead just as fast as I can, driven by the knowledge that the book is desperately needed."

Ornithologists in Florida and other states were noticing the decline in bald eagle and brown pelican populations. It was suspected that DDT washed into the water and contaminated the fish these birds consumed. The adult birds did not seem to be affected, but their eggs were breaking during incubation because of extremely thin shells.

Many challenges met Rachel Carson that summer of 1959 as she began the enormous undertaking of researching and writing *Silent Spring*. Roger had reached school age and needed much of her time. Her book began to take far longer than she had dreamed, realizing that it must be built on an unshakable foundation. By 1960, she had drafted separate chapters on birds and wildlife, groundwater, soil, insect resistance, and cancer. She had begun the difficult chapters on cell biology and genetic mutation. So she was particularly devastated that at the peak of her rhythm, she became ill. There was also the foreknowledge that she would be personally attacked and ridiculed. In retrospect, the completion of her book seems a miracle. As Rachel exposed the world of irresponsible pesticide application, her own body was fighting the demon of metastasized beast cancer.

Even before *Silent Spring* was published in 1962, there was strong opposition to it. As *Time* magazine recounted in 1999:

> Carson was violently assailed by threats of lawsuits and derision, including suggestions that this meticulous scientist was a "hysterical woman" unqualified to write such a book. A huge counterattack was organized and led by Monsanto, Velsicol, American

Cyanamid— indeed, the whole chemical industry—
duly supported by the Agriculture Department as
well as the more cautious in the media.

Anticipation was high as the book neared completion. Supreme Court Justice William O. Douglas, an ardent naturalist, wrote her asking when it would be finished. Chemical companies publicly denounced the content and threatened to stop the publication through legal action. She was personally criticized for being an unmarried woman who had overstepped her bounds. Carson and the environmental movement were and continue to be— criticized by some conservatives who argue that restrictions placed on DDT have caused needless malaria deaths. Many critics repeatedly asserted that she was calling for the elimination of all pesticides despite the fact that Carson had made it clear she was not advocating the banning or complete withdrawal of helpful pesticides; she was encouraging their responsible and carefully managed use with an awareness of the chemicals' impact on the entire ecosystem. In fact, she concludes her section on DDT in *Silent Spring* not by urging a total ban, but with "Practical advice should be 'Spray as little as you possibly can' rather than 'Spray to the limit of your capacity'…Pressure on the pest population should always be as slight as possible."

When the *New Yorker* printed a condensed three-part version prior to publication, President Kennedy read it and began a governmental investigation. Rachel's words had the foundation of impeccable research. Her colleagues knew that no one was more gifted or courageous to sound this alarm.

Finally in September of 1962, *Silent Spring* was published and available in bookstores, quickly rising to number one on the *New York Times'* best-seller list. Rachel was interviewed by Eric Sevareid in her home for *CBS Reports*. Prior to the broadcast, the network received 1,000 letters of protest and three of the network's chemical-based sponsors withdrew their advertising. Rachel's composure and competence were apparent in every moment of the interview. Television allowed Rachel—not her critics—to define the issue of the interrelationship between all living things and their environment. In a single evening, this broadcast had added the environment to the public agenda.

In June of 1963, Rachel was asked to testify before two Senate Committee hearings. The room quieted when the senator from Connecticut cleared his throat and began his well-rehearsed paraphrase of Abraham Lincoln's remark on meeting Harriet Beecher Stowe: "Miss Carson, we welcome you here. You are the lady who started all this. Will you proceed?" This was the moment she had hoped for long before *Silent Spring* was finished. Rachel believed in her vision intensely and had accepted the responsibility to bear witness. Here was the opportunity to mold public policy and shape a powerful social movement that would alter the course of American history.

Silent Spring was translated into twelve languages. Rachel Carson showed the public that they were capable of questioning the government's motives and could establish both local and national policy when it came to health and safety. As Rachel's worldwide influence grew, her own health continued to decline. She secretly fought her cancer with both traditional and experimental treatments. She did not live to see the banning of DDT in United States. Rachel Carson died of cancer on April 14, 1964, at the age of fifty-six.

Rachel Carson knew the importance of what she was doing. Many considered her a prophet. In 1980, she was posthumously awarded the Presidential Medal of Freedom, the highest civilian honor in the United States. In fighting against the poisoning of the earth, she was standing up for everything she most valued. Somewhere she found the strength for this final effort.

Thank you Rachel, for standing up against insurmountable odds to show us what it means to bear witness.

Did you know?

Mangrove Forest—Mangroves (generally) are trees and shrubs that grow in saline coastal habitats in the tropics and subtropics. The word is used most broadly to refer to the habitat and entire plant assemblage or mangal, for which the terms mangrove swamp and mangrove forest are also used.

Red Tide—The term "red tide" is often used in the United States to describe a particular type of algal bloom common to the eastern Gulf of Mexico and is also called "Florida red tide." The density of these organisms during a bloom can exceed tens of millions of cells per liter of seawater, and they often give the water a deep reddish-brown hue.

Fire Ants—Sometimes referred to as simply red ants, fire ants are stinging insects of which there are over 280 species worldwide.

Explore the Land that Influenced Rachel Carson

The Coastline of the Florida Keys

The Florida Keys is an archipelago in the southeast United States. They begin at about fifteen miles south of Miami and extend in a gentle arc south-southwest and then westward to Key West, the westernmost of the inhabited islands, and on to the uninhabited Dry Tortugas. The islands lie along the Florida Straits, dividing the Atlantic Ocean to the east from the Gulf of Mexico to the west. The southern tip of Key West is just ninety-eight miles from Cuba.

Web Site: www.fla-keys.com

Historic Bok Tower Sanctuary

Historic Bok Sanctuary comprises the botanical gardens, the Singing Tower (with carillon bells), Pinewood Estate, Pine Ridge Trail, and a Visitor Center.

Located at 1151 Tower Boulevard, Lake Wales, Florida.

Web Site: www.boksanctuary.org

Reference and Recommended Readings

www.rachelcarson.org

Under the Sea Wind, 1941, by Rachel Carson.

The Sea Around Us, 1951, by Rachel Carson.

The Edge of the Sea, 1955, by Rachel Carson.

The Sense of Wonder, 1965, by Rachel Carson.

Silent Spring, 1962, by Rachel Carson.

The Sense of Wonder, 1965, 1998: published posthumously, by Rachel Carson.

Since Silent Spring, 1970, Frank Graham Jr.

The House of Life—Rachel Carson at Work, 1993, Paul Brooks.

Always, Rachel: The Letters of Rachel Carson and Dorothy Freeman, 1996,edited by Martha Freeman (granddaughter of Dorothy Freeman).

Rachel Carson—Witness for Nature, 1997, Linda Lear.

Lost Woods: The Discovered Writing of Rachel Carson, 1999, Linda Lear.

Courage for the Earth: Writers, Scientists, and Activists Celebrate the Life and Writing of Rachel Carson, 2007, by Peter Matthiessen.

Marjorie Harris Carr

March 26, 1915 (Boston, Massachusetts)–October 10, 1997
(Gainesville, Florida)

I am an optimist. I also believe that Floridians care about their environment. If they are educated about its perils, if they are never lied to, they will become stewards of the wild places that are left.

Marjorie Harris Carr

Saving Florida rivers was Marjorie Harris Carr's passion. She taught us that as citizens of any region we have the power to save what is in our own backyard. The Ocklawaha River in central Florida was Marjorie's focus. Once wild, this river was dammed in the 1960s to make way for a massive public works project called the Cross Florida Barge Canal.

Marjorie was influenced by the natural world of Florida as a child, studied zoology as a scholar, and traveled the world with her husband, Archie Carr, the world-renowned sea turtle researcher. Yet she chose the battle of her life at home. Marjorie exemplifies her connection with nature in this quote:

> Why fight for the Ocklawaha River? The first time I
> went up the Ocklawaha, I thought it was dream-like.
> It was a canopy river. It was spring-fed and swift. I was
> concerned about the environment worldwide. What
> could I do about the African Plains? What could I do
> about India? How could I affect things in Alaska or

105

the Grand Canyon? But here, my God was a piece of
Florida ... a lovely natural area, right in my backyard
that was being threatened for no good reason.

Marjorie Harris was born in Boston, Massachusetts, on March
26, 1915. Marjorie's father, Charles Harris, was a retired Boston
schoolteacher determined to raise oranges in his retirement. As a
result of this desire, her parents moved to Bonita Springs in 1923.
Marjorie was raised in the 1920s on the spectacular and remote
coastline of Bonita Beach, near Fort Myers. Both of her parents
were naturalists who as, Marjorie stated, "knew the answers to the
questions I had about the natural world." It was here she gained her
appreciation and love of the wild beauty of Florida as she galloped
her horse, Chiquita, over the pristine shoreline. She rode the length
of the beach lined with Indian mounds and jumped in the waves.
She also observed the lessons of wildlife destruction. This was the
era of shooting anything that moved. One could paddle down
the Imperial River from the Bonita to the gulf and not see a living
thing—not an alligator, not a cardinal, not a heron. This soulful
childhood connection of beauty tempered with fragility would
guide Marjorie to her life's work.

A gift of $500 from an aunt sent her off to begin her studies at
the Florida State College for Women, now Florida State University.
Marjorie graduated with a B.S. in zoology in 1936. At the time,
Florida was an incredible wilderness, an undiscovered frontier for
scientists. In her foreword to *Ecosystems of Florida*, she writes, "a
graduate student could select a set of animals to work on and
realize that he or she was the first to focus on that particular group
in Florida."

Marjorie also writes that the ability to "read" a landscape
provides the kind of pleasure that comes from knowledge of Bach
or Shakespeare or Van Gogh. Marjorie felt this was a pleasure that
increased with one's knowledge and understanding of the ecology
of Florida and would last an entire lifetime. After graduation, she got
a job as a wildlife technician with a fish hatchery that was part of the
Resettlement Administration, a New Deal organization. The facility

was located at Welaka. She became the federal government's first female wildlife technician. Here she encountered the captivating Ocklawaha River.

A year later, in 1937, she met Archie Carr, a zoologist at the University of Florida. Three dates assured them of their bond. Married for fifty years, they had five children and made a home for their family on Wewa Pond in the woods near Micanopy. Archie's work took them to the habitats of Africa, Costa Rica, and Honduras. Two of their children were born in Honduras. Marjorie assisted Archie from 1968 to 1980 in the long-term research of nesting and remigration of the Atlantic green sea turtle in Totuguero, Costa Rica. Marjorie and Archie created a powerful partnership of love and dedication to the pursuit of scientific conservationism. This commitment influenced four of their five children to choose conservation as their career.

In 1947, Marjorie received her Master's of Science in Zoology from the University of Florida. Her thesis, which was later published, dealt with the breeding habits, embryology, and larval development of the large-mouthed black bass of Florida. The scientific knowledge of this subject would prove important in her fight to free the Ocklawaha River.

Marjorie's work on behalf of the environment started in Gainesville in the early 1960s. She was a member of both the local Audubon Society and Garden Club. Marjorie and other members of the Garden Club initiated the Payne's Prairie Wildlife Refuge. In the early 1960s, the refuge was only as wide as the right-of-way for US Highway 441. The group landscaped the entrance to the Prairie, planted cabbage palms along the road's route, and created viewing areas. This small beginning has now culminated into the Payne's Prairie Preserve, 19,000 acres of wild Florida.

Marjorie initiated a very unique photography contest dealing with Florida landscapes. This competition selected photographs on the basis of their success in picturing the intangible aspects of Florida's environment. It was judged by prominent photographers from around the country and was the first such photography contest ever held in the United States.

Her greatest battle was just on the horizon. In 1570, Governor Pedro Menendez de Aviles, the first Spanish governor of Spanish Florida and the founder of St. Augustine, thought a canal from the gulf to the Atlantic would help Spain conquer the continent. As soon as Florida became a state, and for years afterward, surveys were conducted to evaluate such a deep-water shipping channel. Congress authorized construction in 1933, and work began in 1935 with a dynamite blast near Ocala only to halt a year later when the project ran out of money. The project resumed in the 1960s with state officials claiming that Florida's canal would be bigger than the one in Panama or at Suez. It would be Florida's "Highway of Gold."

In 1962, the Alachua Audubon Society of Gainesville invited two representatives of state and federal agencies to give a talk on the probable effects of the Cross Florida Barge Canal on Florida's environment. The talk was well presented and well rehearsed. The citizens in attendance blanketed the representatives with questions concerning the economics of the project and what effects construction would have on the geology, hydrology, and ecology of the canal project area. The government speakers had no satisfactory answers.

In 1969, members of the Audubon Society with Marjorie Harris Carr and others founded Florida Defenders of the Environment and challenged the project. She stated emphatically, "if we can't save the Ocklawaha, we can't save any lovely piece of this Earth." This group of scientists and other concerned citizens wrote a carefully researched scientific report called the "Environmental Impact of the Cross Florida Barge Canal with Special Emphasis on the Ocklawaha River System." Marjorie, in partnership with Bill Partington, organized and directed this group of professionals to prepare this report, which provided the fundamental information necessary to assess the impact of the barge canal on the river valley. This impact statement, one of the first such reports written by any citizen group in the nation, and with work being done in the Everglades, was a motivating factor in the creation of the National Environmental Policy Act in the early 1970s.

In 1970, the Florida Defenders of the Environment entered into a suit with the Environmental Defense Fund to stop the Cross Florida Barge Canal project. A federal judge issued an injunction and stopped construction in January of 1971. Three days later President Nixon halted all work on the Cross Florida Barge Canal, citing potential serious environmental damage.

Throughout all of Marjorie's battles, she clung to the principle of making environmental decisions based on sound scientific and technical information. During her thirty-year presidency of the Florida Defenders of the Environment, Marjorie followed the precepts of sticking only to the facts and not engaging in emotional attacks in the complex, delicate, and long-term work of environmental protection. She was known by the government representatives she confronted to always be polite and informed— even when she was taking an argument apart piece by piece. When she called Tallahassee to speak with the governor or any other official, she always got through. In November of 1990, President Bush signed the barge canal de-authorization into law.

Harriet Beecher Stowe was an early champion of the Ocklawaha ecosystem, speaking out in print against killing birds and the "war of extermination waged on our forests." Her torch of protection had been handed to another brilliant and determined woman. Today, the land along the Ocklawaha is the centerpiece for one of Florida's most ambitions greenways, the Marjorie Harris Carr Cross Florida Greenway Land Bridge. Designed after the ecoducts of the Netherlands, this corridor stretches across the state from the mouth of the Withlacoochee River on the Gulf of Mexico to the St. Johns River, providing safe passage for hikers, equestrians, off-road cyclists, and wildlife.

But even twenty years after her victory, Marjorie Carr continued to fight to remove the Rodman Dam and let the Ocklawaha run free. Her chief opponents were bass fishermen, led by Florida state representatives who champion the sport. The reservoir obliterates sixteen miles of Ocklawaha, but is revered by the fishermen because it is full of trophy-size bass. Marjorie, who knows the subject so well from her thesis, describes the Rodman Dam "an abomination."

In 1987, as her husband Archie battled cancer, the couple began compiling a list of his writings suitable for his uncompleted project, a book on Florida. Marjorie started to edit a half-century of his writings both previously published and unpublished about the natural history of Florida. The twenty-five chapters were published seven years later, in 1995, as *A Naturalist in Florida: A Celebration of Eden.* Marjorie writes in her preface: "I do not think I am biased when I claim that Archie knew more about Florida wildlife and wilderness than any other person, today or in times gone by."

Marjorie Harris Carr was inducted into the Florida Women's Hall of Fame in November of 1996 at the age of eighty-one. While connected to oxygen and fighting emphysema, she used the phone and her Rolodex as she continued to fight to free the Ocklawaha River.

A year later, in October of 1997 "The Lady of Rivers" died. The army of citizens she inspired to make a difference continues her fight.

Thank you Marjorie, for showing us that our love of nature can be transformed into an effective tool to save what is in our own community.

Did you know?

Cross Florida Barge Canal—A canal project to connect the Gulf of Mexico and the Atlantic Ocean across Florida for barge traffic. The planned route of the canal followed the St. Johns River from the Atlantic Coast to Palatka, the valley of the Ocklawaha River to the coastal divide, and the Withlacoochee River to the Gulf of Mexico.

Indian Mounds —Prehistoric Indians of Florida left hundreds of mounds used for ceremonial and practical purposes.

Canopy River—A river shaded by the uppermost level of a forest formed by the tree crowns.

Atlantic Green Sea Turtle—All species of sea turtles are threatened or endangered. One of the most important nesting grounds for the green turtle population can be located in Tortuguero in Costa Rica.

Archie Carr—In honor of his efforts, the Archie Carr National Wildlife Refuge covers the beaches from Melbourne Beach south to Wabasso Beach. In 1994, the Dr. Archie Carr Wildlife Refuge was established in Costa Rica in his memory.

Explore the Land that Influenced Marjorie Harris Carr

Marjorie Harris Carr Cross Florida Greenway

Crossing central Florida from the Gulf of Mexico to the St. Johns River is the state's premier greenway. This 110-mile corridor traverses a wide variety of natural habitats and offers a variety of trails and recreation areas where visitors can experience the wonders of Florida in their own recreational style.

Web Site: www.dep.state.fl.us/gwt/cfg/default.htm

Paynes Praire Preserve State Park

Located ten miles south of Gainesville, Florida, it contains over twenty distinct biological communities that provide a rich array of habitats for wildlife, including alligators, bison, wild horses, and over 270 species of birds.

Web Site: www.floridastateparks.org/paynesprairie

Recommended Readings

A Naturalist in Florida, 1996, Archie Carr (Marjorie Carr).

Reflection

Great women are still exploring Florida ... and making a difference as a result. Our connection to nature gives us the strength and clarity to nurture the land and to also affect humanity. It is no less important to reach out to our community as it is to champion a global cause. As nature touches us, so may we gently carry this gift into all that we do.

I am continuing this journey of finding the stories of GWEN. Feel free to contact me at linda@itsournature.com.

Artists Acknowledgment

Linda Renc, a calligrapher and artist from Safety Harbor, Florida, has been a specialist in hand-lettering for over thirty years. With a B.A. in graphic design from University of Illinois, she first worked as a freelance commercial artist, progressing into fine art with a focus on calligraphy. Linda has exhibited in juried shows, taught calligraphy, and traveled the United States and Britain to study with international teachers. Linda and her husband, Bill, own The Painted Fish Gallery in Dunedin, Florida, where they are close to the natural beauty of the Gulf Coast.

Bill Renc is a painter in oils and watercolor, with a background in drawing and etching. Bill grew up in Florida, where landscapes, fish, and wildlife became his inspiration. He exhibited in juried shows for twenty years and won top awards in graphics and painting. He also creates original artworks on commission for special events. Bill's artworks are in private collections from Maine to Miami, and in a number of museums and corporate collections. Bill and Linda have a daughter, Chris, who is an artist with an established career in the museum field.

Shari Umpstead is an environmental photographer based in St. Petersburg, Florida. She specializes in environmental portraiture, using natural light to bring out the best in her subjects. Shari was born and raised in Michigan where her parents gave her a Kodak 110 Instamatic at the age of 8. Each summer her family traveled to National Parks giving Shari the opportunity to photograph nature. She credits her parents for teaching her the importance of the environment and appreciation of the beauty of nature. Shari continues to photograph nature and landscapes in addition to her portraiture work and is involved with various environmental groups and causes. Shari met me at Fort DeSoto County Park in St. Petersburg for a fun morning of capturing the perfect picture for GWEN's back cover.

Photo Credits

Harriet Beecher Stowe
Portrait painted in 1853 by Alanson Fisher
State Library and Archives of Florida

Mina Miller Edison
In 1931 the Trail Blazers (an organization made up of some of the original participants in the Tamiami Trail road project of 1923, which linked Miami to Tampa) sponsored a project to beautify the trail (US 41). This included planting trees along the trail in Estero. Mina Edison participated in the ceremony by planting the first cajeput tree in the project. (Source: *Fort Myers Press*, April 5, 1931)

Marjory Stoneman Douglas with her classic wide brim hat addressing an audience
State Library and Archives of Florida

Zora Neale Hurston
State Library and Archives of Florida

Myrtle Scharrer Betz with her dog on Caladesi Island
Photo by permission of Terry Fortner

Marjorie Kinnan Rawlings with her dog at Cross Creek
State Library and Archives of Florida

Anne Morrow Lindbergh in the cockpit of the *Lockheed Sirius* in 1933.
Smithsonian Institution

Jacqueline Cochran
State Library and Archives of Florida

Rachel Carson
   Rachel Carson and Bob Hines Conducts Marine Biology Research in Florida, 1952
      US Fish and Wildlife Service

Marjorie Harris Carr
   State Library and Archives of Florida

LaVergne, TN USA
13 September 2009
157702LV00005B/2/P